Revolutionaries, REBELS & ROGUES of Rhode Island

Revolutionaries, REBELS & ROGUES of Rhode Island

M.E. REILLY-MCGREEN

THE
History
PRESS

Published by The History Press

Charleston, SC 29403

www.historypress.net

First published 2011

Manufactured in the United States

ISBN 978.1.60949.139.0

Reilly-McGreen, M. E.

Revolutionaries, rebels, and rogues of Rhode Island / M.E. Reilly-McGreen.

p. cm.

Includes bibliographical references.

ISBN 978-1-60949-139-0

1. Rhode Island--Biography. 2. Rhode Island--History--Anecdotes. 3. Revolutionaries--
Rhode Island--Biography. 4. Rogues and vagabonds--Rhode Island--Biography. 5. Pirates--
Rhode Island--Biography. 6. Men--Rhode Island--Biography. I. Title.

CT258.R45 2011

974.5'0430922--dc22

2011013958

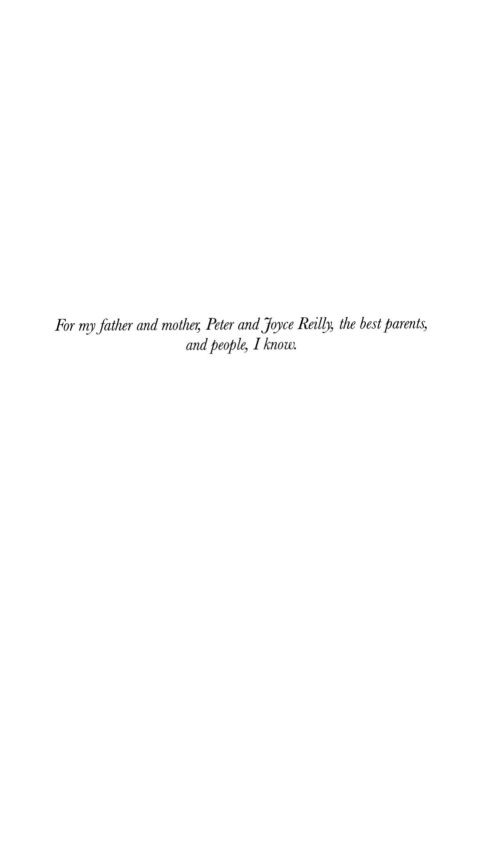

For my father and mother, Peter and Joyce Reilly, the best parents, and people, I know.

Contents

Acknowledgements

M any people made this book possible. I want to thank the staff of the Peace Dale Library. Wakefield is so lucky to have you. Also, thanks go to another town treasure: Betty Cotter; thank you for your wisdom, your knowledge and for the tale of Danny Walsh, one of my favorite Rhode Island bad boys.

Thank you, too, to the History Press crew, especially Jeffrey Saraceno, Ryan Finn, Katie Parry and Dani McGrath. You are all are amazing.

To the team at Embolden: you are all wicked awesome. It's a privilege to work with such a great group of people.

To my family and friends, thank you for always being so supportive and loving. I am reminded constantly how blessed I am in all of you.

To my sons, Reilly, Colin and Peter: you make me proud every day. I love you guys.

And to Joseph: you have my heart. Thank you for being you.

A Series of Fortunate Events

While I had the idea for this book long before Rhode Island's midterm elections of 2010, three election-related events reinforced its central message: Rhode Island is a rebel's state.

WHAT'S IN A NAME? EVERYTHING!

In July 2010, the state legislature decided to put before its constituents the choice to trim the state's formal name of State of Rhode Island and Providence Plantations to State of Rhode Island. Some Rhode Islanders, like myself, were displeased. For starters, we derive a certain pleasure in the fact that the country's smallest state has the biggest name. I imagine it's like what owners of tiny dogs with big barks feel.

The well-intentioned proponents of the bill said that the use of the word "plantations" in the state's name conjured the specter of slavery. Okay, I can see their point. Opponents of the bill pointed out, though, that in 1663, our Puritan founders had no thoughts of slavery but rather ones of godliness and unity when naming the Ocean State. To them, Providence was a synonym for God, and "plantations" meant colonies or settlements. So "Providence Plantations" likely meant "God's community."

Rhode Island good and true,
Our fond hearts cling to you,
You are as pure as morning dew
And fair as your own violet blue.

"VIOLET"
RHODE ISLAND
STATE FLOWER

STATE CAPITOL, PROVIDENCE, RHODE ISLAND

A Rhode Island postcard. *Author's collection.*

When I think of the State of Rhode Island and Providence Plantations, then, I think about the moment when Massachusetts Bay Colony exiles Roger Williams, Anne Hutchinson, Mary Dyer and others got word that England had recognized Rhode Island with a royal charter. The charter guaranteed that residents would have no fear of being "molested, punished, disquieted or called in question for any differences in opinion in matters of religion." Basically, Charles II was saying that you could do whatever you wanted, be whomever you wanted and hold whatever religious views you wanted—you know, as long as you paid your taxes and recognized his sovereign authority.

It could be argued, then, that the name of State of Rhode Island and Providence Plantations connotes freedom. I subscribe to that view. And I, along with nearly 78 percent of the state's voters, said no to the measure that would have meant divorce for the State of Rhode Island and Providence Plantations. A nearly 350-year marriage is worth fighting for.

One final point: the "livlie experiment" in religious freedom that is the State of Rhode Island and Providence Plantations set a standard that our country upholds to this day. As a country, we pride ourselves on our tolerance. To revise our state's name would be to undermine a pivotal

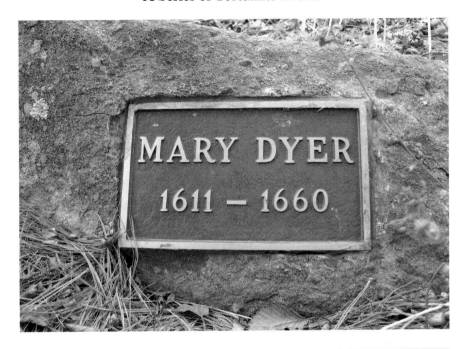

Above: The Mary Dyer Memorial at Founders' Brook Park, Portsmouth. *Photo by author.*

Right: Portsmouth Compact marker at Founders' Brook Park, Portsmouth. *Photo by author.*

moment in our country's history. Seriously. History is ephemeral, and the ephemeral is fragile. Historians will tell you that if a historic place is destroyed, so, too, are the stories about it. It is intolerant to refuse to acknowledge the original, and innocent, intent behind the name. And it would be a grave disservice to Williams, Hutchinson and Dyer. They were freedom fighters. They all accepted exile and, in the case of Dyer, death, rather than recant their belief that people should be free to think what they would and speak to their truth.

It was asking too much of Rhode Island to set aside such auspicious beginnings, not only for our state but for our country, as well.

Take Your Endorsement and...

An even bigger headline-maker of the 2010 campaign season was a certain politician's choice words for President Barack Obama. Gubernatorial hopeful Frank T. Caprio earned his place in infamy for his "Shove it" comment when questioned about President Obama's failure to endorse his candidacy. To be specific, Caprio said that's what Mr. Obama could do with said endorsement.

Caprio was thought to be the frontrunner in the governor's race before the comment was made. Afterward, things got bad. Really bad. Caprio not only lost the election but also came in third, after a Republican in this, the most Democratic state in the country. The lead story in the November 5 edition of the *Providence Journal* put it plainly: "Caprio Undone by Democratic Voters." Lincoln Chafee, the winner, owed Caprio, the *Journal* claimed: "The former Republican can also thank traditionally Democratic labor halls, and the Democratic White House, and another 'Independent Man,' conservative radio talk-show host John DePetro, whose interview with Democratic rival Frank T. Caprio elicited the defining phrase of the campaign: 'Shove it.'"

Democratic Rhode Islanders rebelling against one of their own? Yes, it happens. Why? Maybe Rhode Island didn't want to be known as the state that told its president what to do with his endorsement. Maybe that was going just a bit too far. Even in Rogue's Island.

GIVE IT UP FOR INDEPENDENCE

And so Lincoln Chafee became the first independent candidate in state history to win the governor's seat. He beat Republican candidate John Robitaille by 8,637 votes, a margin of 2.5 percent. Chafee, son of Senator John Chafee, one of the state's most beloved politicians, ran with a simple slogan: "Trust Chafee." Arguably the most compelling of Chafee the Younger's campaign ads was the one featuring footage of his famous father, who holds an almost sainted position in the secular world of politics.

Already a man of enviable lineage, independent Governor Chafee now finds himself associated with another esteemed figure: Rhode Island's *Independent Man.* Permanently installed atop the statehouse, this eleven-foot-tall, five-hundred-pound, classically modeled bronze sculpture has been struck by lightning twenty-seven times. Still he points his spear to the heavens. Is it a gesture meant to taunt gods or inspire mortals? In art, it's always a question of perspective. Arguably, though, Chafee will feel a kinship with this sentinel of freedom and independence that stands atop the statehouse on Smith Hill—especially after Chafee weathers political tempests of his own.

While Governor Chafee's relation to the *Independent Man* is unique, I would argue that it is not exclusive. Every man profiled in *Revolutionaries, Rebels and Rogues of Rhode Island* resembles the *Independent Man* in some fashion. And we claim them all for our own. We admire Roger Williams, Cato Pearce and Edward Everett Hale for their independent spirits. We aspire to create art in the vein of Gilbert Stuart, Henry James and H.P. Lovecraft. We delight in the successes of Samuel Slater, Oliver Hazard Perry and even Danny Walsh. And we treasure pirates Charles Harris and William Kidd for their swashbuckling and sometimes murderous natures.

Rhode Island has weathered nasty criticism from outsiders who have cast it as provincial, insular and corrupt—a place that lionizes its villains. Only recently was it stripped of the title "armpit of New England." Evidently Bridgeport, Connecticut, now wears that crown. What those outsiders don't know, though, is that we wear our wackiness with pride. And we embrace all kinds.

We are the Ocean State. We are a "livlie experiment."

We are an American success story.

Part I
Revolutionaries

EDWARD EVERETT HALE: MATUNUCK'S MYTHMAKER

Writing teachers tell their students that the process of writing must be reward enough for what they do. Write to learn. Write to share. Write to know, they say. Let go of the dual fantasies of fame and fortune. Because, really, seizing J.K. Rowling's throne probably isn't in most writers' futures.

What happens, though, when celebrity comes to someone who doesn't appear to want it? If you're J.D. Salinger, you retreat to New Hampshire and arm yourself with guns and guard dogs.

If you're Edward Everett Hale, you head to Matunuck Beach.

Reverend Edward Everett Hale's *The Man Without a Country*, published in 1863, earned him a permanent position in the American literary canon. It is the fictitious story of one United States Army officer, Lieutenant Philip Nolan, who in anger at the moment of his court-martial says, "Damn the United States! I wish I may never hear of the United States again!" He gets his wish. Nolan's punishment is to be imprisoned for the remainder of his life at sea, on ships, and no one aboard is ever allowed to say the words "United States" in his presence.

In the book's introduction, Van Wyck Brooks wrote, "The story was intended to teach the lesson that a man must have a country, that one cannot throw over the claims of the life in common; and the story met

Above: Hale House, Matunuck. *Photo by author.*

Left: Hale House is now a museum maintained by the Pettaquamscutt Historical Society. *Photo by author.*

the taste of the patriotic public in the Civil War and continued to meet this taste for generations. The story and the hero were entirely imagined, but Hale's Philip Nolan became a sort of national myth."

There are those who say that Hale's contribution to the cultivation of national pride is equal to that of contemporary and fellow Rhode Islander Julia Ward Howe, who had penned the lyrics of "The Battle Hymn of the Republic" two years earlier in 1861. What distinguishes the two, though, is Hale's apparent aversion for literary celebrity. *The Man Without a Country* was published anonymously. Of this, Hale later said, "In private I [made] no secret of my writing *The Man Without a Country*. It was forged in the fire, and I think its great popularity is due to its subject."

Publicity stunt? Unlikely. The Unitarian minister shunned the spotlight. His literary accomplishment would certainly have made him a welcome addition to the Newport literary crowd—of which Howe was a prominent member—but Hale avoided that scene. Hale, who in later years bore more than a passing resemblance to Walt Whitman (not a look society types would have found tolerable), wanted nothing to do with the Newport scene. Instead, he chose to make his summer home, now called Hale House, in Matunuck, which he called "a kind of temple consecrated to Nature."

There Hale lived a Thoreau-like lifestyle with his wife and children. "It is beyond language how much I enjoy this place," he wrote in an 1877 letter to his wife.

Hale called *The Man Without a Country* a "sensation story" containing a "national moral." Readers of the book cannot possibly miss the author's patriotic intention in writing such a composition during the Civil War, when this young nation faced its greatest challenge: preserving its unity.

Hale said of it, "This story was written in the summer of 1863, as a contribution, however humble, towards the formation of a just and true national sentiment, a sentiment of love to the nation."

Hale on Education, Society and Success

Hale did not go the way of many contemporary bestselling authors in following up, and cheapening, his success with variations on a theme. There was no *The Woman Without a Country* or *Chicken Soup for the Man*

Without a Country in Hale's future. *The Man Without a Country* wasn't even his favorite book. Hale thought 1874's *In His Name* to be his best effort.

The no-nonsense Unitarian minister would certainly be appalled at today's celebrity culture. That people could get sillier than Newport society would likely have been unimaginable to Hale. Once called the "busiest man in Boston," Hale's downtime was spent with his family, reading, contemplating nature and conversing about the political and intellectual events of his day.

The minister is credited with more than a few notable and acerbic comments, the subjects ranging from society—"as I have said, I hated society"—to how to talk, how to write and how to be of use in the world. It's not hard to imagine him holding court at Hale House, delivering cultural commentary with wit and humor, looking more salty fisherman than dignified clergyman. A few gems follow.

On How to Talk: In the second volume of *The Life and Letters of Edward Everett Hale*, Edward Everett Hale Jr. gives his father's six maxims: "Tell the truth"; "Do not talk about your own affairs"; "Confess ignorance"; "Talk to the person who is talking to you"; "Never underrate your interlocutor"; and "Be short."

On Success: "The making of friends who are real friends is the best token we have of a man's success in life"; "If you have accomplished all that you have planned for yourself, you have not planned enough."

On Personal Responsibility: "I am only one, but I am one. I cannot do everything, but I can do something. And I will not let what I cannot do interfere with what I can do."

H.P. Lovecraft: Tales of the Outsider

Once upon a time in Providence, there lived a little boy named Howard who thought he was a monster. Howard's mother told him so. She told the neighbors and strangers, too. She would sigh and say that he was,

French signs on the Shunned House's gatepost warn passersby of a strange dog. *Photo by author.*

well, different. A bright, precocious boy to be sure, but a worrisome one, too. He didn't sleep. He didn't eat. Oh, she was proud of him—he was a genius. He was a terribly gifted writer. He would be famous someday.

But he was a burden, too. Imagine having a child so physically repugnant that you had to hide him. Howard, she said, was too hideous to be seen in public. And Howard believed his mother. She loved him, after all. She was saying it for his own good, certainly. Why would he doubt her?

When Howard's mother told him that monsters hovered about their house, he may have believed that, too. Certainly monsters stalked young Howard. They kept him up at night. They would watch him from the shadows, biding their time. Then with the darkness, they would advance:

slinking, stretchy things whose shadows pooled and spread across the floor like seeping blood, and small, invisible things making mad clawing noises as they scurried and scrabbled their way in the spaces behind his bedroom walls. Sleep brought no peace to the little boy. Then the "Night-Gaunts" would come for Howard in his dreams. Silent, crypt-dwelling, faceless demons, these black, rubbery things with their pointed tails would clutch the boy round his stomach and spirit him off "through infinite leagues of black air over the towers of dead and horrible cities," he wrote in adulthood. "They would finally get me into a grey void where I could see the needle-like pinnacles of enormous mountains miles below. Then they would let me drop."

Howard Phillips Lovecraft would never break free of the Night-Gaunts' grasp. Lovecraft's night terrors became his waking thoughts, and he devoted his adult life to writing tales of writhing, tentacled creatures, the very sight of which drove the beholder to madness. It's hard to tell in a Lovecraft story whether the author identified more with the monster or

The haunted basement of the Shunned House. *Photo by author.*

The Shunned House
at 135 Benefit Street,
Providence. *Photo by author.*

the man. Like his monsters, Lovecraft dwelt largely in darkness, preferring
the company of a black cat to that of most human beings. He hated
blacks, Jews and foreigners. Lovecraft made little effort to find regular
work and would likely have been destitute if not for the financial aid of
two spinster aunts. The author ate out of cans and proudly proclaimed
that he could feed himself on pennies a day. He sought out lonely, vaguely
menacing places to wander alone in the dead of night.

Was he a misanthrope? Or were his habits those of a person fearful
that, for him, all human interaction would end in rejection? The likely
answer is both in equal parts. Consider what Lovecraft had to say about
realistic fiction:

> *I could not write about "ordinary people" because I am not in the*
> *least interested in them. Without interest there can be no art. Man's*

relations to man do not captivate my fancy. It is man's relations to the cosmos—to the unknown—which alone arouses in me the spark of creative imagination. The humanocentric pose is impossible to me, for I cannot acquire the primitive myopia, which magnifies the earth and ignores the background.

He must've been a hoot at cocktail parties.

When Lovecraft died—and some might be secretly satisfied to learn that he died a slow, painful death from cancer—he, like Herman Melville and Henry James, believed himself a failure.

But Lovecraft was wrong. In death, the tall, thin and awkward Lovecraft would become a literary giant. Critics would place him alongside the often equally unlikable Edgar Allan Poe; some would even say that he was the better writer of the two (that would be the French). "Though Poe is far more renowned than Lovecraft…both writers have had an incalculable influence on succeeding generations of writers of horror fiction, and Lovecraft is arguably the more beloved by contemporary gothic aficionados," wrote Joyce Carol Oates in the *New York Review of Books* article titled "The King of Weird."

Yes, Oates says "beloved." Lovecraft is worshiped, in fact, venerated as a revolutionary in the horror genre. Stephen King argues, "Now that time has given us some perspective on his work, I think it is beyond doubt that H.P. Lovecraft has yet to be surpassed as the twentieth century's greatest practitioner of the classic horror tale."

Born to Privilege, Heir to Madness

Lovecraft was born in August 1890 to a genteel Providence family. His grandfather, Whipple Phillips, was a wealthy businessman who took in the three-year-old Lovecraft and his mother, Sarah, called Susie, after the death of Lovecraft's father in 1893. Lovecraft's father, a salesman, died of general paresis, dementia brought on by syphilis, in a hospital for the insane. Lovecraft thrived in his grandfather's house, specifically in his library, where he discovered the works of the Grimm brothers, Jules Verne, Dryden, Pope and Ovid. A precocious child, a five-year-old

Lovecraft was removed from his Sunday school class after questioning the existence of God.

Lovecraft eventually left public school. His attendance record was spotty from elementary school onward. In his younger years, mother Susie ostensibly withdrew him because of his susceptibility to sickness. He suffered from facial tics, stomach pains, headaches and bladder issues, but scholars suspect that the symptoms were manifestations of Lovecraft's psychological issues, as Curt Wohleber noted in his article "The Man Who Can Scare Stephen King." Lovecraft left high school after the death of his grandfather and the discovery that the family fortune was lost to bad business deals. During this time, Lovecraft suffered something akin to a nervous breakdown. Wohleber wrote: "The loss of the family fortune and Lovecraft's precarious mental health rendered his dream of attending Brown University an impossibility. He became a recluse, sleeping by day, writing by night. His mother, whose sanity was slipping away, did nothing to stop Lovecraft's withdrawal from society."

Lovecraft did seek public acknowledgement in one area, though. He wanted to be a published writer and submitted scientific articles to local newspapers. But it was a series of letters and verse criticizing another man's erotic writing that launched Lovecraft's professional career. Edward F. Daas, a member of the United Amateur Press Association, invited him to join the organization, and soon Lovecraft was publishing essays and verse in various amateur publications.

Friends made during this time encouraged Lovecraft to write science fiction, a genre he had dabbled in early on. "The Tomb" and "Dagon" established Lovecraft as a science fiction writer and launched what would be a recurrent theme in his work: that of the outsider battling for his sanity. Lovecraft's body of work would indicate that he felt more at home with monsters and aliens than people. In one of his most famous short stories, "The Outsider," the protagonist escapes a subterranean prison and excitedly crashes a party, eager to befriend those there. They flee in terror, though, and the hero is driven mad when, upon catching sight of his reflection in a mirror, he realizes that *he* is the monster.

Visits From the Night Gaunt

Providence residents Muriel and C.M. Eddy Jr. were friends and fans of Lovecraft's. In the Eddys' book, *The Gentleman From Angell Street*, Muriel says that she and her husband corresponded with Lovecraft for more than a year before a face-to-face meeting—though they lived in the same city. Such was the power of Susie. "There is no doubt that Sarah Lovecraft was a possessive mother who meant to keep Howard tied to her apron strings as long as possible," Muriel wrote. It was only after Susie died in 1921 that the friends met in person. Susie Lovecraft, like her husband before her, went mad and died in Butler Hospital on May 24, 1921. For the first time in his life, Lovecraft was free of his mother. Or was he? It is interesting to note that Lovecraft was a friend and mentor to *Psycho* author Robert Bloch.

Did the specter of Susie Lovecraft hold sway over her son like Mother Bates did Norman? Possibly. Despite regular correspondence and real proximity, the first meeting of the Eddys and Lovecraft only happened after Susie's death.

Though Muriel Eddy had great admiration for Howard, she admits that he was kind of weird: "Although the day was insufferably hot, his hands were cold, almost clammy; and I recall wondering how anyone's hands could be so frigid in an atmosphere of almost a hundred degrees."

The guy didn't sweat. He was a fussy dresser. And he spoke of his aunts' care of him in a way that was juvenile, telling Muriel:

> *I live with my two devoted aunts...They let me sleep all hours of the day, if I am so inclined. Most of my nights I spend in writing...My aunts are two of my best critics...They listen attentively when I read my manuscripts aloud to them, offering suggestions, praising and criticizing my work alternately. I'll admit sometimes my characters make the good ladies shiver. But by this time they are used to my style of writing.*

The last bit of Lovecraftian weirdness that Muriel shared concerned the horror writer's reaction to her opening a can of salmon for her cat: "When Lovecraft saw the salmon, he repressed a shudder and passed a hand over his forehead as if he suddenly felt faint. That was the first inkling I had that fish or seafood in any form actually made him ill. Even the sight of fish distressed him beyond description."

Terrified of tuna. Scared silly of squid. Yet the same man would walk three miles in the dead of night to visit his friends, for after that first meeting, Lovecraft asked and was granted permission to call on the couple after 11:00 p.m. He would stay until two o'clock in the morning and then walk home.

On one occasion at the Eddys' home, Lovecraft performed a dramatic reading of another of his more famous tales, "The Rats in the Walls." Muriel, who just might have had a crush on the cold and clammy Lovecraft, praised the performance:

> *Lovecraft could very easily have become an actor, because he read the manuscript with real effect. He imitated the characters, taking on the voices as he pictured them, and it was all I could do to stand it! I could feel the gooseflesh rising all over my body! He even laughed the insane laugh of the cannibalistic character, adding to the horror of the whole thing.*

It's Not Easy Being Greene

Muriel downplayed her shock to learn of Lovecraft's 1924 marriage to Sonia Haft Greene by mail. Lovecraft had made no mention of Greene when he announced to the Eddys that he was moving to New York just a few months earlier. The ardent anti-Semite also neglected to tell them that he was marrying a Jewish woman. It was a short-lived affair, Muriel noted:

> *I hesitate to say much about the marriage of Sonia and Howard, except that I believe they were both (in the long run) most bitterly unhappy... Rumor had it that Sonia wanted him to "commercialize" his work... to put it on a sound money-making basis, and to this the man objected strongly. His forte lay in the writing of weird tales and revising for others, and because of the strain on his nerves he became a real introvert.*

Wait. It was Greene's fault that he *became* an introvert? *He* suffered strained nerves? Greene married a man who didn't work and who had the nerve to tell her that only Aryans were to be invited to the house. How's that for a strain on the nerves?

Lovecraft's racism wasn't the cause of the breakup, though. Nor was money, despite the fact that Lovecraft didn't make any. Sonia, a successful businesswoman, seemed happy enough to support him. The demise of the marriage was likely because Lovecraft was too weirded out by the normalcy of it all. His out came when he received an invitation to return to Providence to visit his aunts in 1926. Sonia would have relocated, but it appears that neither Lovecraft nor his aunts wanted her to do so. The divorce was finalized in 1929.

Lovecraft resumed his friendship with the Eddys, but it seems that most other relationships were maintained by mail. Letters written late in his life indicate that Lovecraft seemed to be letting go of some of the phobias and the ethnocentricity that had so marginalized him. Lovecraft's real enemy was always himself. He was the outsider. To read him is to be assured that the man battled real and imagined demons as potent and deadly as the vampire in 1924's "The Shunned House." The story, set in the basement of a house that still stands at 135 Benefit Street, contained a "vaporous corpse-light, yellow and diseased, which bubbled and lapped to a gigantic height in vague outlines half human and half monstrous… It was all eyes—wolfish and mocking," with a "rugose insect-like head."

Wow. The guy must've slept with the light on.

Lovecraft died at forty-six of colon cancer and Bright's disease. He was buried in the family plot at Providence's Swan Point Cemetery. Only a few people attended his funeral. Some time after his death, Lovecraft's fans would pool their money to buy him a headstone, which reads, "I am Providence." Would Lovecraft have wanted such an egotistical epitaph? The ex-wife would probably say no. Or was he the type enamored of being a loner? You be the judge: in a 1916 letter, Lovecraft wrote that

I am never a part of anything around me—in everything I am an outsider…But pray do not think, gentlemen, that I am an utterly forlorn and misanthropick creature…Despite my solitary life, I have

found infinite joy in books and writing…A sense of humour has helped me to endure existence; in fact, when all else fails, I never fail to extract a sarcastic smile from the contemplation of my own empty and egotistical career!

OLIVER HAZARD PERRY: "WE HAVE MET THE ENEMY AND THEY ARE OURS"

Naval war hero Oliver Hazard Perry lived a mythic life. Too bad its lines paralleled those of Achilles.

Perry's military service began when he was thirteen. He won a midshipman's appointment on the U.S. frigate *General Greene*. True, Perry's father was captain of the ship, but those who would cry nepotism were

A statue of Oliver Hazard Perry at Washington Square, Newport. *Photo by author.*

likely silenced by the boy's dedication. By the time Perry received his first command, at age twenty-four, of the fourteen-gun schooner *Revenge*, he was a war veteran who had tangled with the infamous Barbary pirates.

Perry's command of the *Revenge*, though, marked a low point in his career. In 1809, the ship ran aground in heavy fog on a reef in Block Island Sound, off the coast of Westerly. An attempt to tow it failed, and the ship sunk. Perry was exonerated in the court-martial that followed, with blame falling on the ship's pilot.

While awaiting new orders, Perry courted and married twenty-year-old Newport resident Elizabeth Champlin Mason in 1811. When a post to a seafaring ship was not forthcoming, a disappointed Perry turned his thoughts to lakes. He wrote to friend Isaac Chauncy, commander of naval operations on the Great Lakes. Chauncey set him up on Lake Erie, building a small flotilla of ten ships. Perry's dreary task turned exciting on September 10, 1813, when six British vessels engaged nine navy ships. In the ensuing battle, Perry became the first commander to defeat a British squadron in the history of the world—and that after losing his first ship to enemy fire. He also became the first American commander to shift his flag from one vessel to another mid-battle. This entailed leaving one ship by skiff and rowing to a second—a very dangerous stunt.

In announcing his victory, Perry uttered words worthy of George Patton—or Charlton Heston in a *Ben Hur* moment: "We have met the enemy and they are ours."

An Omen Dismissed?

Where Perry is concerned, the comparison between heroes real and imagined would not be complete without mention of Shakespeare's *Julius Caesar*. In the play, Caesar's wife Calpurnia foretells her husband's death after dreaming of it. Perry's wife, Elizabeth, also had an ominous dream of her husband's demise but dismissed it, saying, "If I were superstitious it would worry me, but I am not, and I shall think no more about it." Elizabeth never saw her husband alive again.

Perry died of yellow fever off the coast of Venezuela on August 23, 1819, on his thirty-fourth birthday. It must have been appalling to Perry when he realized that he would die of something so puny as a mosquito's prick. Achilles probably had the same dying thought about Paris.

There are two footnotes to Perry's story. First, his body was not returned to Newport until seven years after his death. The prevailing thought was that to transport a diseased corpse was to endanger the crew. So Perry was buried at Port of Spain, Trinidad. The U.S. government ordered it retrieved, and the remains were interred at Newport's Old Common Burial Ground, according to a biography found on the Redwood Library and Athenaeum website. Ten years later, the remains were unearthed again for reinterment in the Island Cemetery. Three burials, two disinterments and not a single allegation of suspected vampirism? Unusual for Rhode Island.

For the second postscript, on January 7, 2011, one day before the 200th anniversary of the sinking of the *Revenge*, two scuba divers announced that they had found the remains of the schooner off the coast of Westerly. At the time of the writing of this piece, local marine biologists have withheld judgment either way.

SAMUEL SLATER: HOW ONE MAN'S REVOLUTIONARY IS ANOTHER'S ROGUE

Samuel Slater was a villain and a hero. A traitor and a patriot. An irredeemable rogue and a respected citizen. It was a matter of perspective—you either loved or hated the guy.

If you were an English citizen, you would likely use the invectives villain, traitor and rogue to describe Slatersville's namesake. If you were a citizen of the newly liberated United States of America, then Slater was the embodiment of the very ideals on which the new republic was built. Drop his name in a roadside tavern about 1795 or so, and people would likely raise a pint and shout "Huzzah!"—a weird little English word meant to describe an exclamation of joy and approbation. It didn't last long in this country—kind of like the monarchy in that way.

So what was so polarizing about Slater? What treasonous deed did he do to turn public enemy? It was not murder, nor bearing arms against his countrymen. It was much, much worse, the kind of crime for which only the rack or a good drawing and quartering would do: industrial espionage.

Sticky Fingers Slater led the United States in a second revolution, safeguarding its independence through economic freedom and earning the epithet "Father of the Industrial Revolution" in the process.

From Apprentice to Industrialist

Samuel Slater was born in England in 1768, the son of a wealthy English landowner. At fourteen, Slater became the apprentice of Jebediah Strutt, partner of Richard Arkwright, inventor of the spinning frame. This tool spun cotton to thread stronger than that made by hand. The spinning frame was too large, though, for hand-operating. so the industrious Arkwright lighted on the idea of using water to power his spinning frame. In 1774, Arkwright was operating his first textile mill powered by water wheel.

After the stunning outcome of the American Revolution, England likely took solace in anticipating economic domination where the colonies were concerned. But Mother England was about to be thwarted again, this time by an upstart whiz kid with a photographic memory and a sewing needle.

Slater spent seven years with Arkwright and Strutt. A condition of working for the pair was that Slater would not divulge anything he learned about the mill's workings. To reveal said secrets or to try to leave England with plans or tools was a violation of law. Samuel Slater decided that the promise of great wealth was worth a little risk. In 1789, his seven-year apprenticeship ended. He had seen a newspaper ad offering $100 to experienced millworkers willing to make the trip to America. Slater obtained what amounted to a fake ID, disguised himself as a farmer and boarded a ship for America. He had sewn his real identification into the lining of his jacket. The plans for a wheel-powered mill he kept in his head.

Once in New England, he sought out Moses Brown, a Quaker who had turned his back on his family's slave trading business and was now intent on building cotton mills in America. Yes, there is irony in an abolitionist building cotton mills. With Brown's money and Slater's brain, a business venture was hatched that would secure America's place in world commerce. Slater and Brown built two Arkwright mills along the Blackstone River in Pawtucket. Soon these two factories were producing more yarn than any other operation in the country.

Child Labor

Slater opened his mill with nine employees. Most were children, ages seven to twelve years. Their weekly salaries were between thirty-five and fifty cents a week. An eighteenth-century workday at Slater Mill lasted twelve hours, and a week was six and a half days long. Children were desired as millworkers. Their size made them better suited to operate some machines than their adult counterparts. Unfortunately, children often were maimed, and some killed, while doing the work. The numbers of children hurt or killed at Slater Mill are unknown; that statistic wasn't considered important enough to record. In fact, mill owners were less concerned with the loss of a child's limb than if the blood and gore ruined the thread, or, infinitely worse, the machine. In her article "The Mill Girls of Lowell," Verena Rybicki wrote of conditions in a Lowell, Massachusetts mill:

> *There were as many as 800 to 1,200 machines in a room, all clanging and clanking in unison. The racket must have been deafening...Steam was constantly hissing into the room, providing the humidity essential to maintain the correct environment for the spinning and weaving of cotton. Windows were sealed shut to prevent the humidity from escaping, and temperatures would hover between 90 and 115 degrees. The window panes were grimed over by a brown deposit, reducing the light so that kerosene lamps would have to be lit—another smell to add to that of machine oil.*

And of the accidents, Rybicki noted:

> *The huge flywheel rotated at 75 miles per hour and if the 900-pound leather belt on it snapped, anyone in line with it was in mortal danger. Shuttles flew across the loom at 90 miles per hour, and if one went*

astray, it might pierce the brick wall to a depth of six inches. Fingers and thumbs were certainly vulnerable to this onslaught.

And the constant inhalation of cotton fibers and other pollution aggravated and weakened the lungs. One respiratory disease, brown lung, was believed to be directly linked to working in the mills. And consumption, now known as tuberculosis, spread easily in an environment so conducive to disease.

Conditions were appalling and the pay, dismal, from a twenty-first-century perspective. It was the norm, however, for children to work from a young age, either on the farm or in the city. Children were employed in mills, factories and even coal mines. It was fifty years from the time of Slater's opening his mill before people would voice their misgivings about child labor. It was one hundred years more before child labor was restricted. The photographs of Lewis Hine and testimonials from the mill children themselves in publications like the *Lowell Offering* moved people, certainly, but it was not until 1938, the year Congress passed the Fair Labor Standards Act, that child labor was, in effect, outlawed.

Slater died in 1835 at the age of sixty-seven, a year before the first strikes of the Lowell Mill girls began. By the 1850s, New England mills were so plentiful that prices fell and discontent rose. Many quit the mills, and immigrants filled their spots.

Give that Man a Jingle

A perennial favorite of elementary school teachers in search of an educational field trip, Slater's Mill wrested *Yankee Magazine*'s coveted 2009 Best History Escape in Rhode Island title from its glitzy neighbors, the Newport mansions. Partial credit has to go to the mill's dedicated docents, men who gladly don breeches and stockings and women who willingly sacrifice cute hair and makeup to give tourists that authentic eighteenth-century mill experience.

Slater's fifteen minutes of fame, though, is due to 1970s Saturday morning cartoons. Cartoon enthusiasts may remember that Slater made a guest appearance on the educational *Schoolhouse Rock!* series of the 1970s and 1980s. The series, which spawned the megahits "Lolly, Lolly, Lolly, Get Your Adverbs Here," "Conjunction Junction" and "I'm Just a Bill," also produced the 1977 jingle "Mother Necessity," a lesser-known but snappy little ditty celebrating American ingenuity. This is Slater's part:

When Robert Fulton made the steamboat go,
When Marconi gave us wireless radio,
When Henry Ford cranked up his first automo,
When Samuel Slater showed us how the factories go,
And all the iron and oil and coal and steel and Yankee don't you know,
They made this country really grow, grow, grow, grow,
With Mother Necessity and where would we be
Without the inventions of your progeny?

Samuel Slater changed a country with his water-powered mill. He employed whole families who might otherwise have been unable to find employment for themselves. But he also set up a system that required child laborers to work long hours in unhealthy conditions for meager wages. Some equated factory work in the North to slavery in the South.

So, does Samuel Slater deserve commendation or condemnation? For the English, the answer is easy. For America, it's not so simple.

GILBERT STUART: IT TAKES AN EGOMANIAC TO PAINT A LEGEND

Since Jesus Christ set the gold standard for humble beginnings with his manger birth, we've come to expect our heroes' career trajectories to follow a particular pattern: modest birth, mythic life. Like Jesus Christ, America's premier portraitist, Gilbert Stuart, had a similar start, if Richard McLanathan's account in his 1986 book, *Gilbert Stuart*, is to be believed: "There, on a bitter cold night, the third of December 1755, he was born in an upper chamber, above the rumbling water wheel and massive gears and grindstone of a snuff mill built beside the runoff from Petaquanset Pond in the sparsely inhabited countryside of North Kingstown County."

Gilbert Stuart's birthplace marker, Saunderstown. *Photo by author.*

Inauspicious births aside, though, there are few comparisons to be drawn between the Son of God and the snuff mill guy's son, although, it must be noted, Stuart might argue otherwise. Modesty was never his thing.

Stuart's early biographers not only forgave him his considerable flaws but also came close to worshiping the guy. Mistaking the work for the man, they described Stuart as heroic, even noble, supremely talented, generous, gregarious and driven, a man whose portraits of America's Founding Fathers gave a nascent country its national identity. Stuart's detractors would likely say that yeah, okay, maybe Gibby Stuart was all of those things, but the guy was also temperamental, stubborn, touchy, irresponsible, sneaky and even, gasp, cowardly.

They were all right. Stuart was all of those things.

How might Stuart answer his critics? He probably wouldn't. Not directly anyway. A polished conversationalist, he'd likely sidestep it with the panache of a seasoned politician, saying something like, "For my own part, I will not follow any master. I wish to find out what nature is for myself, and see her with my own eyes. This appears to me the true road to excellence."

Who's gonna argue with that?

Gilbert "Gibby" Stuart was the third child and namesake of snuff mill owner and operator Gilbert Stuart and his wife, Elizabeth Anthony. He was born in the residence attached to the snuff mill on what is now Gilbert Stuart Road in Saunderstown. Stuart would delight patrons and friends by describing the location of his birthplace as "six miles from Pottawoone and ten miles from Pappasquash and about four miles from Conanicut and not far from the spot where the famous battle with the warlike Pequots was fought."

People thought that Stuart had been born in India, McLanathan noted. Stuart probably liked that. More exotic. The mill produced snuff, pulverized tobacco leaves that colonials would insufflate, which usually entailed mounding the powder on the finger and snuffling with the nose—a "pernicious, vile dirty habit, and, like all bad habits, to be carefully avoided," Stuart is said to have told an acolyte. He would know. Stuart was a big-time snuffer.

The Stuart family left the Saunderstown mill for Bannister's Wharf in Newport when Stuart was six. There the family doctor noticed the young boy's artistic talent and got famed painter Cosmo Alexander to give the boy painting lessons. Stuart would eventually travel to Europe with Alexander, who made his living painting portraits of wealthy people. Stuart liked Alexander's lifestyle and decided that he, too, would paint for a living. He returned to Newport briefly after Alexander's unexpected death in 1772 but set sail for London in 1775, following his friend Benjamin Waterhouse, a medical student. It seems that the future painter of patriots was immune to the call of patriotism himself.

Once in London, Stuart was disappointed to learn that his friend had left London for Edinburgh. Stuart knew no one in London. In what was at once an act of desperation and an excellent strategic maneuver, Stuart wrote a letter to another American painter in London, Benjamin West. Recollection of the letter must have caused Stuart some embarrassment later in life, both for its spelling and syntactical errors, as well as its plaintive, self-pitying tone:

Gilbert Stuart Birthplace & Museum, Saunderstown. *Photo by author.*

Pitty me Good Sir I've just arriv'd att the age of 21 an age when most young men have done something worthy of notice & find myself Ignorant without Bussiness or Freinds, without the necessarys of life so far that for some time I have been reduc'd to one miserable meal a day & frequently not even that, destitute of the means of acquiring knowledge, my hopes from home Blasted & incapable of returning thither, pitching headlong into misery.

And it keeps going. No doubt Stuart's situation was dire, but it needn't have been so dismal. At twenty-one, Stuart's prima donna tendencies were already in place.

As Stuart was writing the letter to West, boyhood friend Waterhouse was attempting to help Stuart. When he heard of his friend's financial troubles, he'd gotten his friend a gig painting the portrait of a doctor, one of Waterhouse's teachers. Amazingly, Mr. Oh-God-I'm-pitching-headlong-into-misery Stuart wasn't interested. Waterhouse was mortified.

In *Gilbert Stuart: Portraitist of the Young Republic*, a 1967 book published by the Rhode Island School of Design (RISD), Waterhouse is quoted as becoming physically sick from the affair.

You see, Waterhouse had collected money from his fellow classmates:

> *They each one paid their half-guinea subscription, and I was unwise enough to let my needy friend have the greater part of it before he commenced the painting, which I never could induce him even to begin. This was a source of inexpressible unhappiness and mortification, which at length brought on me a fever, the only dangerous disease I ever encountered. After I recovered I had to refund the money, which I had not a farthing of my own.*

While the friendship would endure, Waterhouse had hit his limit. He'd already bailed his friend out of debtor's prison twice before this. Lucky for Stuart, West came through. The twenty-four-year-old painter took his fellow American in, and Stuart lived with the family for five years. West, history painter to King George III, proved to be Stuart's ticket to fame. In the Royal Academy exhibition of 1782, Stuart displayed his portrait *The Skater*, and his reputation as an artist solidified. His skill as a portraitist eclipsed West's. Historians say that West took pride in his assistant's success, calling him "the best portrait painter in the world." Stuart could've taken a lesson or two from his teacher where graciousness was concerned. He reportedly said of West, "He never could paint a portrait."

Stuart would go on to set the standard in Europe for portrait painting. He gravitated to military men, and while Stuart was a realistic painter, his male subjects often had the gravity and assurance of mythic characters. Women didn't fare as well, McLanathan noted: "There were few women sitters because his drive toward realism didn't allow for the expected flattery." In the days before Photoshop, women relied on their portraitists to play down, if not ignore altogether, their physical flaws.

Despite his great success, Stuart had money problems. He was a prolific painter, but his profligacy routinely exceeded his earnings. He had to flee London for Dublin in 1787 to escape fed-up creditors. Then, in 1793, Stuart fled Dublin for New York, though this time it was not creditors but rather the threat of a French invasion that spurred Stuart to leave the country.

Back in his homeland, Stuart made the acquaintance of John Jay, chief justice of the Supreme Court and signer of the United States Constitution. Commissions soon came Stuart's way. There was General Matthew Clarkson, General Horatio Gates, Major-General Henry Dearborn and Judge William Cooper. Stuart's reputation grew and with it his already substantial ego. In John Lennon–esque fashion, Stuart boasted, "In England, my efforts were compared to those of Van Dyck, Titian, and other great painters—here they are compared with works of the Almighty."

And Then Came the Portrait

It seemed fated that Stuart should paint George Washington. No painter in America was Stuart's equal and, arguably, no man was Washington's. It must have been an intimidating experience, though, even for a man of Stuart's considerable ego. Stuart's recollections of Washington support this assumption. In his book, McLanathan quoted Stuart, saying of Washington's features, that they

> *were totally different from what I had observed in any other human being. The sockets of the eyes, for instance, were larger than what I had ever met with before, and the upper part of the nose broader. All his features were indicative of the strongest passions, yet, like Socrates his judgment and self-command made him appear a man of different cast in the eyes of the world.*

Then again, what might've looked like singular self-command could've just been boredom on Washington's part. He hated sitting for his portraits. Stuart painted Washington in 1795 and 1796.

Washington's wife, Martha, and other family members found the likenesses somewhat lacking, but in fairness, Stuart did his country a great service, wrote E.P. Richardson in the RISD volume. "Stuart's portraits of Washington are not merely the best known; they are Washington in the minds of most of his countrymen," Richardson noted. Stuart was charged with painting a myth, for Washington had been elevated from "a noble and interesting man—into a demigod, a sentimentalized pious hero, a white marble statue."

Thomas Jefferson, James Madison, James Monroe and John Adams would also sit for Stuart. No doubt Stuart had stories about each, but Adams's 1826 portrait deserves special attention. Adams's portrait was, Richardson wrote, "an old man painted by an old man." Stuart was about seventy and Adams, ninety. Adams, like Washington, was not a fan of sitting for hours to have his portrait painted, and at his advanced age, the process could even have been painful. But he liked Stuart, saying:

> *Speaking generally, no penance is like having one's picture done. You must sit in a constrained and unnatural position, which is a trial to the temper. But I should like to sit to Stuart from the first of January to the last of December, for he lets me do just what I please and keeps me constantly amused by his conversation.*

No small praise from Adams, who was not known for holding back criticism. Just ask Thomas Jefferson.

The Adams portrait attests that Stuart's talent stayed with him into old age, despite his suffering from gout, tremors and paralysis late in life. He died just two years after completing it. This time, the portrait drew extravagant praise from the sitter's family members. Josiah Quincy wrote, "[T]his portrait of John Adams is a remarkable work, for a faithful representation of the extreme age of the subject would have been painful in inferior hands. But Stuart caught a glimpse of the living spirit shining through the feeble and decrepit body."

Then there was this from Washington Allston: "Called forth from its crumbling recesses, the living tenant is there—still ennobling the ruin, and upholding it, as it were, by the strength of his own life. In this venerable ruin will the unbending patriot and the gifted artist speak to posterity of the first glorious century of our Republic."

Stuart must have loved the reviews. As for that "ruin" of a man, the "feeble and decrepit" Adams? Probably not so much.

Cornelius Vanderbilt: "I Got the Power"

In Cornelius "Commodore" Vanderbilt's hands, business became a revolutionary act.

The nineteenth-century railroad baron and shipping magnate is credited with inventing the modern corporation. In revolutionizing transportation, he changed America and embodied the promise of capitalism.

"Overachiever" is too underwhelming a title for such a man. In his day, Vanderbilt was the barometer by which other tycoons were measured. As such, he was alternately revered and vilified, a robber baron of the same ilk as J.P. Morgan, the Rockefellers, Andrew Carnegie and the Astors.

Cornelius Vanderbilt.
Library of Congress.

There are myriad books and essays on Cornelius and the Vanderbilt family, often described as Newport's First Family. In the interest of full disclosure, Commodore Vanderbilt didn't live in Newport. Nor did his children. It was the third generation of Vanderbilts who were responsible for the building of the Breakers and the Marble House.

So why include the Commodore here? Vanderbilt's venerable name and vast fortune—as well as his descendants' appetite for over-the-top architecture—cemented the island's reputation as America's society capital. The Vanderbilt name and Newport, the City by the Sea, are irrevocably entwined.

What follows are fun facts, did-you-know snippets to stump the docents at the Breakers.

A Cornelius Vanderbilt Primer

- Vanderbilt was a go-getter. He started his first business at sixteen, borrowing $100 from his parents to buy the sailboat necessary to run his ferry and freight business between Staten Island and New York City. In his first year of operations, the teenager was able to repay the loan plus $1,000, his parents' share of the profits that he had made.

- The Commodore didn't care much for organized religion or formal education. Of the latter, Vanderbilt famously said, "If I had learned education I would not have had time to learn anything else." Like the playwright George Bernard Shaw, Vanderbilt favored phonetic spelling, using "no" to mean "know," for example.

- He changed the way a country traveled. Vanderbilt became a millionaire first in steamship service. In the 1860s, he foresaw the advantages of rail travel and began buying railroads. The New York Central Railroad was the result. After five years in the railroad business, the Commodore was $25 million richer.

- He had a thing for his cousins. In the tradition of Edgar Allan Poe, Cornelius Vanderbilt did not look far for a mate. Both of

Vanderbilt's wives were also his blood relatives. His first wife, Sophia Johnson, was his first cousin. They had twelve children. In 1869, a year after Sophia's death, Vanderbilt married distant cousin Frances "Frank" Armstrong Crawford. Vanderbilt was seventy-three and Frank, thirty-nine. Seven of Vanderbilt's children were older than their new stepmom. Vanderbilt scholars say that this second marriage gave the Commodore more vigor.

- He had a thing for pretty spiritual healers, too—Miss Tennessee Clafin, in particular. Vanderbilt's healer, spiritual medium and maybe mistress was also enterprising. Clafin and her sister, Victoria Woodhull, claimed to have opened the first female-run brokerage house on Wall Street, thanks to Vanderbilt's support. What kind of trading went on in the house is anyone's guess. There are no books of business or financial records to examine and no evidence that Vanderbilt had any hand in the matter.

- He was the Bill Gates of his day. When Cornelius died in 1877, his estate was worth $100 million.

- He loved one of his children more than the others—if money was a measure of his love, that is. Son and senior manager of the business William H. Vanderbilt inherited the bulk of his father's estate, $95 million, which would be valued today at about $26 billion. The other nine surviving children each got $500,000. As you might imagine, there was a little tension, followed by a big lawsuit lasting more than two years. The nine lost. Their shares would "only" be worth $130 million today.

- He wasn't the forgive-and-forget type. Crossing Vanderbilt was a dangerous gamble. He once said, "You have undertaken to cheat me. I won't sue you, for the law is too slow. I'll ruin you."

- He may have inspired one of the biggest techno hits of all time. Vanderbilt said, "What do I care about law? Ain't I got the power?" More than one hundred years later, the German group Snap! recorded an international hit in "The Power," the refrain of which is "I Got the Power."

- He became a philanthropist late in life. After his second marriage, Vanderbilt reversed his position on education. Likely yielding to his second wife's wishes, Vanderbilt made a gift of $1 million to Nashville, Tennessee's Central University. Today that would amount to $260 million. Central University wisely changed its name to Vanderbilt University.

GOVERNOR ISAAC WILBOUR AND THE WRETCH AT THE WHIPPING POST

Oftentimes, to be judged a criminal in colonial America was to face a harsh sentence. Early Americans approached their law enforcement with the same zeal they had for their religion.

Take flogging, the act of beating, lashing or whipping a barebacked individual with a cane or whip, for instance. Early Americans added to the pain and humiliation of the victim by carrying out penance publicly. And women, as you might guess, suffered greater humiliation than men. The Puritans of the Massachusetts Bay Colony, for instance, would flog a Quaker by stripping her to the waist, binding her to work animals, like oxen, and whipping her as she was dragged through the street. What worse punishment could a modest God-fearing woman face?

That thought must have run through the minds of some of those who gathered that fateful day in 1806 near the John Almy House at Tiverton Four Corners to see a half-naked woman flogged. The woman's name and her crime have been lost, but the details of her day of reckoning have been assiduously recorded. It was a history-making day, a first salvo fired at the patriarchy. And Rhode Island governor Isaac Wilbour found himself in the heat of the fray. For the very sight of the poor wench stirred local women into such frenzy that they accosted the governor. And what happened next toppled an institution.

Governor Wilbour had taken Great West Road upon his return home from business that day. At Tiverton Four Corners, he witnessed a woman, half-naked and tied to a whipping post. The condemned woman was wailing, as would be expected. What likely took the governor by surprise, though, was the number of women gathered around her who were also wailing, screaming and crying. Only the men were quiet, noted David Patten in an article entitled "Those Four Corner Ladies" contained in the 1976 book *A Patchwork History of Tiverton, Rhode Island*. They were loitering about "more interested in the shapeliness of the victim's back than in the outrage about to be visited upon it."

The governor's progress did not go unnoticed by the crowd. The women surrounded Wilbour and his horse, preventing his going any farther. The state's highest-ranking official likely got a tongue lashing as injurious to the spirit as the woman's would be to her back. The women, Patten wrote, demanded that the governor stop the proceedings, saying that to be publicly flogged "for just a little carrying on—that surely was going too far."

Wilbour was in a difficult position. The sight of a woman about to be flogged must have offended his Quaker sensibilities. After all, Quakers had been flogged, branded and banished from the Massachusetts Bay Company for their beliefs. One of the most famous of the sect, Mary Dyer, a former island resident, had been martyred. But the law was the law, and he was sworn to uphold it.

Wilbour told those gathered that state law dictated such a punishment be carried out for conviction on a misdemeanor. He added that it was his duty as governor to see the punishment executed. Finally, he withdrew from his coat a book of Rhode Island law and read: "The condemned shall be tied to an upright post and flogged according to the sentence of the court."

An *upright post.*

Did he stress the words? Did he wink? Was the honorable Governor Wilbour at all responsible for what happened next? The quick-witted women of Tiverton saw a loophole. If the post were toppled, then the sentence could not be carried out.

Patten described the scene that followed:

> *Like angry bees they swarmed upon the victim who had misdemeaned. They unbound her from the post and drew the habiliments of modesty over her admirable back and shoulders. And then—ah, what cannot*

womanhood do when its righteous fury is aroused!—they puffed and they huffed until that post was no longer upright. It slanted over, and presently, there it lay, prone upon the ground, never to rise again, the very form and symbol of injustice brought low.

The governor is said to have witnessed the vandalism with a wry smile. Certainly the scene made an impression on him. For no woman was ever flogged in Rhode Island again.

It would be forty-two years before New York's Seneca Falls Convention forced the nation to consider the issue of women's suffrage. Two years later, the National Women's Rights Convention in Worcester, Massachusetts, demonstrated that the right to vote was no passing fancy or whim of the "weaker" sex.

At the time of the incident at the whipping post, the Nineteenth Amendment was 114 years in the future. Governor Wilbour saw, though, that there was an advantage to appeasing the women, even though he would never benefit from a single female vote in his political career. Perhaps, though, the women's outrage appealed to his better nature. Or maybe he subscribed to a simpler truth: when the woman of the house is happy, everyone else is, too.

Part II
Rebels

The Death of Chief Canonchet, North America's Most Fearsome Rebel Warrior

As he bared his neck for a beheading, Narragansett Chief Canonchet might have thought, "What more?" The United Colonies (Massachusetts, Plymouth and Connecticut) had stolen his lands, burned his home and murdered his people, and now they were about to take his life. He had been the victim of betrayal; many of his fellow Native Americans had turned foe, taking the colonists' side in King Philip's War.

Canonchet was the most revered and fearsome warrior in New England, and yet he sought to remain neutral in this latest conflict with the colonists. Canonchet had fought hard for peace; he'd hoped to keep his people, the Narragansetts, out of the war. He had been a constant and true friend to Roger Williams and the other white people who'd been exiled from Massachusetts. His friendship with Williams was one characterized by mutual respect and a shared tolerance for customs and practices different than one's own. His people had saved Roger Williams and his family from almost certain death when they had wandered into Narragansett Bay territory that winter of 1636.

Why wasn't a history of peaceable living enough to alleviate the colonists' fears of Indian predations? Canonchet's people were the ones who should have been fearful after the atrocities committed at the Pequot fort in Mystic and at Canonchet's own encampment in the Great Swamp. Indian warriors expected to die in battle, but they hadn't anticipated that the colonists would take the fight to their elders, women and children. Who did that sort of thing?

As the Mohegan Oneco, the son of the man who'd killed Canonchet's father, prepared to deliver the death blow, was Canonchet consumed with hatred, fear or malice? Did he call on his gods to curse the men? No. He had hope. He hoped that his death would spur his remaining Indian brothers to fight harder and rally around King Philip in his effort to preserve his people's ways.

While Canonchet lost his life and Philip the war, their examples endure.

Narragansett chief Canonchet was beheaded on April 2, 1676, in Stonington, Connecticut. His crime was his refusal to surrender all Narragansetts who had participated in the rebellion known as King Philip's War. The fourteen-month contest between the United Colonies and those Native Americans who refused to submit to English rule is considered one of the bloodiest conflicts in the history of the country. Historians call Canonchet's death heraldic, the first in a series of events that marked the end of the conflict and the demise of the Native American way of life.

"The Deadliest War"

King Philip's War, a conflict that began in early summer of 1675 and ended in late summer of 1676, has been called the deadliest war in American history. At its nexus were the Wampanoags and their leader, Philip (or Metacom), whose relationship with the European transplants had completely broken down for more than one reason. Several years earlier, colonists had forcibly taken Philip's older brother, Alexander, to Plymouth to get his signature on a document promising continued peaceable relations between the two groups. It didn't go so well. Alexander died while in the company of the colonists. Philip also found himself answering to accusations of planned insurrections against the English made by the Mohegans and the Narragansetts. Still, Philip tried to maintain amicable relations with the European settlers, even as they took his land for their houses and fences and their grazing livestock destroyed his crops. The mysterious death of a Natick Indian, John Sassamon, in 1674 damned Philip, however. Sassamon had reported that Philip intended to wage war against Plymouth, a threat that authorities initially did not take seriously—the prevailing sentiment was that no Indian could be trusted. Sassamon left Plymouth saying that Philip would kill him if he were to learn that the Natick Indian had revealed the Wampanoags' intention to wage war.

Sassamon did turn up dead. Colonists fished his body out of the ice at Nemasket's Assawompset Pond. Another Native American claimed that three Wampanoags loyal to Philip had committed the murder. The Plymouth court found the three guilty and executed them. James D. Drake claimed in his book *King Philip's War: Civil War in New England, 1675–1676* that these executions had a symbolic meaning for Philip. The colonists were Christianizing the native people, and loyalties were shifting. King Philip saw Christianity as a threat to his power. Drake wrote: "On the eve of the war, he [Philip] lamented to John Easton of Rhode Island that 'all English agreed against them [the Wampanoags].' The colony of Plymouth had not fulfilled its reciprocal political relationship with the Wampanoags. The world that Philip believed he had created had disintegrated."

The metaphorical disintegrating world was about to become horrifically literal and draw many reluctant Native Americans into the fray, Canonchet included. Philip and his Wampanoags attacked Swansea on June 24, 1675. Nine colonists were killed.

Canonchet would have less than ten months to live.

The Great Swamp Fight

At one thousand acres, South Kingstown's Worden Pond is the largest natural lake in the state. It's the kind of place that inspires painters to set up easels and poets to scribble in notebooks. Local folklore says that it is a favorite fairy haunt, and you can see its appeal: the tall marsh grasses and thick vegetation would afford the intrepid pixie protection. The beaver, muskrat and marsh birds also make their homes there. Baby turtles are

A view of the Great Swamp, West Kingston. *Photo by author.*

fond of sunning themselves on the rocks and branches that break the lake's surface. In the summer, wildlife must bear windsurfers skittering across the lake's placid surface; in the fall it's the canoeists' turn.

In the final days of June 1675, Roger Williams traveled to a spot near Worden Pond to meet with Narragansett leaders and ask them not join in the fight. Williams was pleased to learn that they had no intention of following Philip into war, and he wrote as much to Connecticut's governor. In six months' time, though, colonists from the United Colonies would breach the Narragansetts' palisade in the nearby Great Swamp and deliver a devastating blow to the tribe.

The Great Swamp Fight took place on December 19, 1675. Believing that Canonchet had violated his own promise of peace with the colonists, more than 1,100 men, including 150 Mohegans and Pequots, overwhelmed the fort, entering through an unfinished portion of the barricade. The colonists set fire to the fort, which contained somewhere between 300 and 1,000 women and children.

The Narragansett warriors, most of whom were likely outside the fort, must have been horrified by the sight. Among the casualties were King Philip's wife and young son. Canonchet had promised Philip to protect them during the conflict. Those who survived the attack fled the swamp to join Philip.

In his 1961 book *Indians, Privateers and High Society: A Rhode Island Sampler*, author Bertram Lippincott quotes a firsthand account of the battle published in the 1912 book *Narration of the Great Swamp Fight*. The unnamed author—and imaginative speller—exonerates himself and his peers of any wrongdoing by turning the massacre into an Almighty-endorsed holy war–esque event, characterizing the colonists as "Sampsons" and the Narragansetts as "Philistines":

The Great Swamp Fight marker, West Kingston. *Photo by author.*

The Great Swamp Fight Obelisk, West Kingston. *Photo by author.*

By these and some of Fugitive Indians our Forces had certain Inteligence where the Enemy lay; although it was Sunday, our Men thought they could not serve God Better than to require Justice of the Indians for the Innocent Blood which had been so oft by those Truccent Savages shed; and we were chearfully ready (as so many Sampsons) to forgo our own lives to be revenged of these Philistines, that had made Sport with our miseries; we marched through the Snow and came to a thick Swamp (i.e. a Quagmiry-Wood) wherein were encamped 3500 Indians.

That a man was able to pause during the heat of battle in a "Quagmiry-Wood" to do an accurate headcount is nothing short of extraordinary. Truly a feat. But back to the author:

We first demanded to have Philip and his Adherents to be delivered Prisoners to us, according to Articles: And had no other Answer but shot; then we fired about 500 Wigwams (i.e. Indian Houses) and killed all that we met with of them, as well Squaws *and* Papooses *(i.e. Women and Children) and Sanups (i.e. Men). In the midst of the Wood was a plain piece of Ground on which the Indians had built a fort; the Stone-Wall whereof enclosed about four or five Acres, in which Rampart was about 1000* Indians; *this Hold we assaulted they within on the first onset stoutly repulsed; But our God, blessed for ever, so prospered and encouraged the* English, *that every one put forth his utmost strength, and on renewing the Assault we became Masters of the place, though with the loss of many of our Brave Chieftains, who sold their lives at a dear rate.*

Yes, these would be the "Brave Chieftains" who killed the "squaws" and "papooses" as God looked on approvingly. He continued:

We were no sooner entered the Fort, but our Enemies began to fly, and ours had now a Carnage rather than a Fight, for everyone had their fill of Blood: It did greatly rejoice our Men to see their Enemies, who had formerly sculked behind Shrubs and Trees, now to be engaged in a fair Field, where they had no defense but in their Arms, or rather their Heels; But our chiefest Joy was to see they were mortal, as hoping their Death will revive our Tranquility, and once more restore us to a settled Peace which (through the Blessing of God) we have long enjoy'd.

The result: "We have slain of the Enemy about 500 Fighting Men, beside some that were burnt in their Wigwams, and Women and children the number of which we took no account of."

Estimates vary as to the number of Narragansett casualties. Professor Drake puts the death totals at 97 Narragansett warriors and between 300 and 1,000 women and children. The colonists fared better. The United Colonies lost 70 men and another 150 were wounded. About 40 Englishmen were buried in a mass grave at Smith's Castle, just outside of Wickford. The grave is marked by a rock bearing a plaque in a tangle of trees and bushes next to Wickford Cove. A monument commemorating the fight can be found in West Kingston. The twenty-foot obelisk and four rocks, each bearing the engraved name of one of the United Colonies and Rhode Island, can be found in a clearing in the woods off Route 2 on Great Swamp Road. There are two engraved stone markers at the side as well. One reads:

> *Attacked*
> *within their fort upon this island*
> *the Narragansett Indians*
> *made their last stand*
> *in King Philip's War and*
> *were crushed by the united forces*
> *of the Massachusetts, Connecticut*
> *and Plymouth Colonies*
> *in the*
> *"Great Swamp Fight"*
> *Sunday 19 December 1675*

The other marker is missing. According to historical records, it read:

> *In memory of*
> *Major Samuel Appleton*
> *of Ipswich, Massachusetts*
> *who commanded the*
> *Massachusetts forces and*
> *led the victorious storm*
> *column at the*
> *Great Swamp Fight*
> *Dec. 19, 1675*

The markers were installed at the site by the Rhode Island Society of Colonial Wars in 1906 and the Rhode Island Historical Society in 1916, respectively.

There is no homage paid to Canonchet at the Great Swamp Fight memorial site. In Narragansett, at the intersection of Strathmore Street

The Indian head sculpture at the entrance to Canonchet Farm, Narragansett. *Photo by author.*

and Route 1A, the entrance to Canonchet Farm is marked by a twenty-three-foot wooden sculpture of an Indian head. Self-taught artist Peter Wolf Toth named the sculpture *Enishkeetompauog Narragansett*, which, roughly translated, means "all human beings at the small, narrow point." Two Narragansett stonemasons, Craig "Little Fox" Champlin and Ellison "Sonny" Brown, constructed the stone base on which the sculpture sits. The thin, worn face of the Indian is arresting. He is both regal and mournful, and while representative of a people and not a person, the sculpture and Canonchet have become connected in the minds of many who have seen the statue. Some even refer to it as Canonchet.

"I Shall Die Before My Heart Is Soft"

What does survive of Canonchet is the tale of a promise made by him to Roger Williams. Though Canonchet did join Philip in warring against the European colonists, he faithfully kept his promise to Williams that the founder's family would not be harmed in the campaign. In the 1877 book *A Short History of Rhode Island*, George W. Greene described the scene:

> *Tradition says that when the enemy approached Providence, Roger Williams, now a very old man, went out to meet them. "Massachusetts," he said, "Can raise thousands of men at this moment, and if you kill them, the King of England will supply their places as fast as they fall." "Let them come," was the reply, "we are ready for them. But as for you, brother Williams, you are a good man; you have been kind to us many years; not a hair of your head shall be touched."*

Though fifty-four houses in Williams's Providence settlement, Williams's included, went the way of Canonchet's Great Swamp fort, the Williams family was spared.

Canonchet and a large portion of the remaining Narragansetts joined Philip in western Massachusetts after the horrors of the Great Swamp. The Narragansett warrior was captured when he returned to Rhode Island to retrieve supplies.

Greene's account of Canonchet's capture reflects the early twentieth-century attitude toward the Narragansetts, in particular, and Native Americans, in general. His narrative—unhampered by attribution to historical record, by the way—seems more like a scene lifted from a John Wayne movie:

> *A young Englishman attempted to examine [Canonchet]. "You much child; no understand matters of war. Let your brother or your chief come. Him I will answer," was his [Canonchet's] haughty reply. He was offered his life if his tribe would submit, but refused it. The offer was renewed and he calmly said, "Let me hear no more about it." He was sent to Stonington, where a council of war condemned him to death. "I like it well," said he; "I shall die before my heart is soft, or I have said anything unworthy of myself." That as many possible of his own race should take part in his execution, Pequots were employed to shoot him, Mohegans cut off his head and quarter him, and the Niantics to burn his body.*

Again, it is worth repeating that Greene does not account for how he came by such details, saying only that "I have spoken kindly of the State of my birth, but mindful of the historian's first duty, I have striven in everything to speak truthfully. It is an unvarnished tale." Guess we have to take his word for it.

Tales of Canonchet's death do vary. Some have him being apprehended by the Mohegans and executed by firing squad. Others talk of his beheading. That one man should suffer so much rage is hard to think about for too long.

Canonchet, King Philip and Pocasset Princess Wetamoo all suffered indignities after death, as well. Each had their heads taken from their bodies and staked by colonists. Canonchet's was sent to the Hartford court that condemned him as a "token of love and loyalty," Greene wrote. What is certain is that those early settlers of the New World had not yet let go of the worst of their Old World ways.

Some cultures believe that a body must be intact to enter the afterlife. Viewed from this perspective, the gruesome acts of dismemberment and decapitation are, if possible, made even worse for their symbolic reference: one people trying to deny another eternal rest.

If they wander still, the spirits of Philip and Canonchet can take some satisfaction in the fact that, though they lost their fight, they died heroes.

Rhode Island's Recovery of the Remains of Major General Nathanael Greene

For 115 years, the remains of Major General Nathanael Greene, Revolutionary War hero and friend and confidant of George Washington, were missing in action. Georgia lost them. (In a situation such as this, Georgia's unofficial nickname, the Goober State, really is spot on.)

Anyway, in 1901, a group of Rhode Islanders—specifically the Rhode Island State Society of the Cincinnati, an association with membership limited to descendants of Revolutionary War soldiers—resolved to find Greene's remains. The members dedicated $100 to the effort and secured permission from Georgia to do something a bit unorthodox: tomb breaking.

Brigadier General Nathanael Greene was George Washington's right-hand man and the only man other than Washington to serve in the Continental army for the whole of the American Revolution. A Rhode Island native, Greene's leadership, unequalled skill as a military strategist and general neatness, where camps and troops were concerned, stood out from other New Englanders, who were "an exceedingly dirty and nasty people," according to Washington.

Washington believed Greene to be a true patriot, a man who put the greater good before personal gain, wrote Charles Caldwell in his 1819 *Memoirs of the Life and Campaigns of the Hon. Nathaniel [sic] Greene, Major General in the Army of the United States, and Commander of the Southern Department, in the War of the Revolution.* Upon his appointment of Greene to the position of quartermaster general of the Continental army, a position that Greene did not want, Caldwell wrote:

> *It was well known to Washington, that the soul of his friend, and favourite* [sic] *officer, was indissolubly wedded, not to the duties of the staff, but of the line. Notwithstanding this, he expressed, in a conversation, on the subject, with a member of congress, his entire persuasion, that, if General Greene could be convinced, of being able to render to his country, higher services, in the quarter-master department, than in the field, he would sacrifice, at once his partialities to his patriotism, and accept the appointment. "There is not," said he, "an officer of the army, nor a man in America, more sincerely attached to the interests of his country." Could he best promote those interests; in the character of a corporal, he would exchange, as I firmly believe, without a murmur, the epaulet for the knot. For, although he is not without ambition; that ambition has not, for its object, the highest rank, so much as the greatest good.*

Clearly such a man should not be lost to history.

And so in March 1901, in service to the great patriot Nathanael Greene, two men, Charles Gattman and Edward Keenan, took pickaxes to the graveyard crypts in Savannah at the Colonial Park Cemetery, the second oldest in the city. It must have been foul, if not creepy, work—dirt, dust and the long, long dead.

In Search of Major General Greene

People had their ideas about what had became of Greene's remains. Gerald M. Carbone writes the following in his 2008 book *Nathanael Greene: A Biography of the American Revolution*:

> *Some said that a woman loyal to the British crown had taken the Revolutionary War hero's bones from her family crypt and tossed them into Negro Creek; others said that his bones had been exhumed from the old Colonial Park cemetery and reburied next to his widow out on Cumberland Island; one old man recalled that as a child he played on a hill said to contain Greene's bones.*

Greene died on June 19, 1786, at the age of forty-three at his estate, Mulberry Grove, located north of Savannah. The likely cause of death was a stroke brought on by prolonged sun exposure. Greene left a wife, Catharine "Caty" Littlefield Greene, and six children. With no marker or record to orient them, the city workers had no choice but to begin breaking into the crypts at Colonial Park. Carbone quoted a March 3, 1901 article that appeared in the *Savannah Morning News*: "A morbid curiosity drew a crowd to the scene. Many of those attracted by the prospect of a peep at the remains of persons who died a century ago did not stay long, the one peep sufficing them, but there were others with no especial interest in the work who remained for hours."

In 1901, no forensic experts could be called on to identify remains. DNA testing was unimaginable. But some of what distinguished Greene in life might have remained in death. The workers were looking for a skeleton measuring six feet—Greene was a big man, especially by colonial standards—and possessing a broad forehead. If said skeleton should have a sword or metal buttons on or about his person, well, that would be pay dirt. Officers sported metal buttons bearing the symbol of an eagle. A soldier's uniform had cloth-covered wooden buttons. Lastly, it was said that Greene's oldest child, George Washington Greene, was buried with him. The younger Greene had drowned at the age of eighteen in a canoeing accident on the Savannah River.

What the Gravediggers Found

By Monday, March 3, Keenan and Gattman had busted into more than a dozen crypts, but none contained the prize they sought. Their luck changed midday, though, upon entering the vault of Lieutenant Governor (and Royalist) John Graham. At first, the old vault appeared to be another red herring, containing the coffin of a man who had died fifty-six years earlier. But one of the men on the scene noticed that there were fragments of a second coffin on the other side of the tomb. Beneath, there was the skeleton of a man—with a uncommonly large skull.

Further examination of the remains yielded a coffin plate inscribed with the date 1786, the year Greene died. A metal button and French silk gloves were unearthed. And then there were the bones of a second skeleton. When the coffin plate was cleaned, all doubt was removed:

NATHANAEL GREENE
Obit. June 19, 1786
Aetat [Age] *44 years*

Carbone noted that the coffin plate is mistaken in one respect: Greene died at the age of forty-three, not forty-four. What is no longer in question, however, is the whereabouts of Greene's remains.

There was some squabbling between Rhode Island and Georgia as to which state had the right to the remains. Greene's descendants ultimately decided that he should remain in Savannah. The war hero and his son were laid to rest in Savannah's Johnson Square, beneath a fifty-foot, white marble obelisk that had been erected in his honor in 1830. According to Visit Historic Savannah (visit-historic-savannah.com), the Marquis de LaFayette was present for the laying of the monument's cornerstone in 1825. At that time, he said of Greene: "The great and good man to whose memory we are paying a tribute of respect, affection, and regret, has acted in our revolutionary contest a part so glorious and so important that in the very name of Greene are remembered all the virtues and talents which can illustrate the patriot, the statesman and the military leader."

It is an impressive monument for a larger-than-life man. While Rhode Island did not win its campaign to see Greene returned home, it did prevail in a larger sense. If not for Rhode Islanders, Greene's remains would likely still be buried in a tomb bearing another's name. The efforts of the Rhode Island State Society of the Cincinnati did more than solve a mystery; they restored a great patriot to his rightful place of honor.

HENRY JAMES: NEWPORT'S PRODIGAL SON

Hands down, there's nothing scarier than a creepy kid, is there?

Henry James knew it and thought to up the ante by giving us a pair of them in *The Turn of the Screw*. But he didn't end there. James made them beautiful, angelic even, as well as pitiable. Imagine him thinking, "Hey, let's take a pair of orphans and put them in the care of a cold, unfeeling uncle who not only doesn't want to be bothered by them but also doesn't want to be reminded of *their existence*. Then let's put them on a lonely estate in the English countryside in the care of a homicidal young governess who may or may not be seeing a couple of malevolent ghosts that may or may not have returned from their graves to claim the two children whom they may or may not have molested in life." Yeah, let's do that.

Then let's leave the reader wondering if the kids are really evil or just innocent wretches, victimized brutally and permanently by every adult they encounter.

Confused? That's Henry James for you. The one-time Newport resident was a nineteenth- and twentieth-century literary lion, delivering such classics as *Daisy Miller, Portrait of a Lady, What Maisie Knew* and *The Wings of the Dove*. He was also a loner, an American who spent much of his adulthood as an expatriate, saying, "I am turning English all over," and, "It is, I think, an indisputable fact that Americans are, as Americans, the most self-conscious people in the world, and the most addicted to the belief that the other nations are in a conspiracy to under-value them."

Self-conscious. Undervalued. Lonely. Alone. Abandoned. You have to wonder, was Henry James really talking about himself? Authors are often caught unpacking their psychological baggage through the characters in their novels. A recurrent theme in James's work is how fresh, young things become despondent, dispossessed adults (that is, if they don't die in the course of the story), and certainly there are similarities between James's life and work.

A morally bankrupt high society is also a recurrent character in James's work, and a corrupted and corrupting Newport makes an appearance more than once in his writings—though James chose Europe as the setting for most of his stories. The Newport of James's youth was remembered fondly by the author, but he renounced the place in adulthood, wrote Deborah Davis in her 2009 book *Gilded: How Newport Became America's Richest Resort*. James, she wrote, "was appalled by the 'gilding' of the city. He remembered when Newport reminded him of 'a little, bare, white, open hand,' charming, inviting, and delicate. He returned to find the same hand vulgar and unattractively stuffed with gold. James despised the marble monstrosities and their socially ambitious occupants."

In the 1902 short story "An International Episode," one of the principal characters, Lord Lambeth, believes that Newport's women will be vapid and easy: "Lord Lambeth had a theory, which it might be interesting to trace to its origin, that it would be not only agreeable but also easily possible, to enter into relations with one of these young ladies; and his companion (as he had done a couple of days before) found occasion to check the young nobleman's colloquial impulses."

In other words, Lambeth had come to the City by the Sea to score. His friend tries to reason with him: "You had better take care," says Percy Beaumont, "or you will have an offended father or brother pulling out a bowie knife."

"I assure you it is all right," Lord Lambeth replies. "You know the Americans come to these big hotels to make acquaintances."

Yes, that's exactly what Newport women do: sit by the sea drinking Del's waiting for the moment they're able to "enter into relations" with foreign men. Spot on.

James's disapproval of Newport may also have been colored by an accident he suffered in 1861 while fighting a fire that consumed six Newport buildings. What happened is unclear. He referred to his injury as "an obscure hurt." The mysterious hurt prevented James from serving in the Civil War and injured his psyche, as well, scholars say. That may have motivated him to write repeatedly about hapless heroines, such as *The Turn of the Screw*'s tortured governess and Daisy Miller, as well as possibly evil/possibly misunderstood children like *The Turn of the Screw*'s Miles and Flora.

Certainly James—who once famously said, "I've always been interested in people, but I've never liked them"—had his issues. But in literature, one person's misfortune is another's entertainment. *The Turn of the Screw* is considered a classic in its genre. Several movie adaptations have been made, including the 2001 film *The Others*, starring Nicole Kidman.

James became a naturalized British citizen in 1915, in part because he was angry at America for its refusal to enter World War I when Britain did. He died of a stroke a year later. Like the characters in his novels, James suffered in his later years. He had tried playwriting and been booed off the stage on opening night. And his later novels were not as popular as his earlier works. Society had shunned him, and James feared that he would not be remembered.

James was well acquainted with futility: "We work in the dark—we do what we can—we give what we have. Our doubt is our passion and our passion is our task. The rest is the madness of art."

In one of *The Turn of the Screw*'s creepiest scenes, the boy Miles delights in scaring his governess, telling her, "Think me—for a change—*bad*!" Lest she misunderstand, he repeats it: "When I'm bad I *am* bad!" and then, "Think, you know, what I *might* do!"

The governess responds with new resolve to save Miles from demonic possession: she ends up smothering him. Maybe accidentally. Defenders would say she hugged him to death.

As goes the governess, so goes Newport. The Queen of Resorts is possessive. Newport suffers James's insults and injuries, even his abandonment, but still she claims her prodigal son. Case in point: James has a permanent place on the Redwood Library and Athenaeum's Newport Notables list—alongside the incorrigible playboy James Gordon Bennett Jr. and privateer John Banister.

That "little, bare, white, open hand" keeps a firm grip on its own.

THE MORSEITES:
GOD'S CHOSEN PEOPLE OR PUBLIC NUISANCE?

Had the first Puritans lived to see the Morseites at worship, they would have thought that the world had indeed gone to the devil. To watch people hooting and hollering as they ran around on all fours—well, that would have caused a God-fearing Puritan to reconvene the Court of Oyer and Terminer faster than a prepubescent girl could cry witch.

But Rhode Island from its inception had billed itself as a safe haven for even the oddest forms of religious expression. When in 1657 the Massachusetts Bay Colony asked Rhode Island Governor Benedict Arnold to banish its Quakers, he politely declined the request and, in doing so, set an enduring precedent. Benedict Arnold wasn't one to bend to the bluster of Massachusetts blowhards, who, by the way, were sending their Quakers to the Ocean State. No, said Arnold to the Massachusetts authorities, we'll not banish your oddballs, your malcontents or your shrews (only he said it much more diplomatically).

Arnold did Roger Williams, Mary Dyer and Anne Hutchinson proud in that moment. And the august governor also set a precedent in terms of how the state deals not only with its citizens but also with pushy outsiders. Where others might try to stifle the freedoms of those who are different, we in Rhode Island champion their individuality and stand in solidarity with them. Even the weirdoes.

And when it comes to challenging the status quo, and general weirdness, few religious sects did it better than the Morseites. Hopkinton—from which so many weird supernatural tales hail, just saying—was home to John Belden in the early part of the nineteenth century, about 1810 or so. He became leader of a short-lived religious sect called the Beldenites. Within this sect was a man named Morse, who broke from the Beldenites to form the Morseites. Morse was more successful than Belden, at least for a time. According to Reverend S.S. Griswold in his *1757 Historical Sketch of the Town of Hopkinton, From 1757 to 1876, Comprising a Period of 119 Years*, Morse, no first name given, even had his own psalm:

Ye Morseites of Hopkinton,
Keep your armor bright;
Ye Morseites of Hopkinton,
Make ready for the fight.

A keeper.

Griswold noted the Morseites were baptized Christians, but that's about the only thing the Morseites and other Christian denominations had in common. The Puritans would have found the Morseites' habit of kissing one another during worship lascivious and wanton. Behavior worse than that of Catholics, even.

Even the shimmying Shakers likely would have kept a safe distance from the Morseites. Sure they danced, but they didn't bark. Griswold writes of the Morseites:

> *These fanatics might have been called very properly religious gymnasts, for in their acts of religious worship, they ran around the chimney, dancing, barking, hooting, leaping, and shouting, sometimes they ran like quadrupeds upon their hands and toes. The families were very affectionate in their devotional exercises, practicing what they called the Holy Ghost kiss.*

A friendly little sect, to be sure, and a forgiving one. Griswold recounted one incident involving the public confession of a man's many sins. No penance for this guy, though. Not a word of reproach. Instead, for the sinner a passionate embrace awaited, Griswold noted:

> *One evening at Mr. Kenyon's house after Mr. Morse had preached, a Mr. Palmer arose and made a very and explicit confession of his numerous evil ways, whereupon Mrs. Kenyon who was sick in her bed arose in her night clothes, and, pressing through the crowd, embraced and kissed Mr. Palmer, evidently with much affection, and then fell down and prayed in her deshabille as she was.*

No mention of Mr. Kenyon's reaction to Mrs. Kenyon's act of Christian charity toward the wicked Mr. Palmer. No doubt other sinners were lining up to get their turn at absolution in the arms of the scantily clad Mrs. Kenyon—that is, the ones who weren't horizontal. Griswold continued: "Some persons lost their strength and fell upon the floor. One woman after falling commenced whirling around on her hip, her clothes and loose hair flying horizontally."

It appears that the Morseites may have invented break dancing.

And how did the Morseites conclude their worship? By caroling. They went house to house, waking people up and warning them to flee the certain wrath to come.

The Morseites did not engender a lot of goodwill among their neighbors. In 1815 or so, the sect packed up and headed for Ohio. And it was never heard from again.

Cato Pearce: God's (And God's Wife and Daughter's) Chosen One

A freed black man living in South County in the early nineteenth century would be lucky to have a steady, manual labor–type job and a modest home. But history tells us that dreamers and innovators routinely ignore the limits that others would impose. The question is: how did they dare to dream?

Might it be adversity? Can a dream be born of pain, as the lash flays the flesh from one's back? Can a dream be formed from the fear of being hunted and enslaved? Do dreams arrive unbidden when one is behind bars?

The latter is true, of course, of Martin Luther King Jr. and Nelson Mandela. And there is also a little-known Rhode Island figure by the name of Cato Pearce.

A former slave and evangelical preacher, Pearce was also an author, despite his inability to read or write at the time of his autobiography's publication in 1842. The anonymous abolitionist who transcribed *A Brief Memoir of the Life and Religious Experience of Cato Pearce, a Man of Color, Taken Verbatim from his Lips and Published for his Benefit* wrote in his introduction that Pearce was "entirely without an education" and "never learned to count one hundred."

We know that the Potter family is buried in Kingston, but what of Cato Pearce? *Photo by author.*

The ghostwriter warns against dismissing Pearce as ignorant, sort of: "I am persuaded that all who know him will bear me witness, that his native intellectual faculties, do not appear below mediocrity."

At fifty-two, Pearce was learning to read and would likely succeed, the ghostwriter noted, for Pearce had a powerful benefactor: "Some things in Cato's experience are truly wonderful; especially what he terms his vision. I fully believe, that the ever blessed God did condescend to *teach* him in that remarkable manner which he sets forth. I believe it was a reality, and not an illusion."

If the abolitionist is to be believed, Pearce, the former slave, is a member of one of the most elite groups in all of human history. Membership is limited to a very few, biblical celebrities like Moses, Abraham, John the Baptist and St. Paul—men to whom God has spoken directly.

Son of Slaves

Pearce was born in 1790 to unnamed slave parents. Only their owners' names merited recording. Pearce's father belonged to James Hazard and his mother to Giles Pearce. Cato Pearce lived with his mother at his master's Wickford home and, as was the custom, bore the surname of the slave owner. Pearce's mother abandoned him and his two siblings when he was just six years old. In his memoir, Pearce recounted his mother telling him to "be a good boy and she would bring me somethin' when she came back."

Pearce's mother's abandonment must have been terrifying. At six, Pearce was the oldest of the children; the youngest was ten months old. Perhaps, though, he came to understand his mother's actions. Pearce's master was not a man averse to capital punishment. At eighteen, Pearce ran away, despite his eventual freedom being all but guaranteed by state law. In 1784, Rhode Island enacted a law that noted that "no person or persons, whether negroes, mulattoes, or others, who shall be born within the limits of this state, on or after the first day of March, A.D., 1784, shall be deemed or considered as servants for life, or slaves." The law promised Pearce's freedom when he turned twenty-one. His freedom was in sight. Why, then, would Pearce run?

The likely answer is fear. When Pearce ran away, he didn't try to cross any borders. Pearce wanted an ocean between himself and his master: "I shipped on board of the schooner *Four Brothers*, Captain Bailey, for Wilmington, North Carolina; never intended to come home any more."

That was not to be. Pearce recalled:

> *The captain said on his return he was goin' into Boston; but the mate was sick, and he therefore went into Wickford, R.I., where he* [the mate] *belonged. We got into Wickford on Sunday; and at the very time my master happened to be out a fishing. He knew it was the vessel I went in, and came on board and took me on shore. He took all my wages, gave me a floggin', and after that I remained with him two years.*

At twenty, Pearce ran away again, this time to Rehoboth, Massachusetts. Pearce took to working for and drinking with Samuel

Lyon, "a dreadful wicked man, and while livin' with him I became more wicked and hard than ever." Pearce stayed three years with Lyon, until the latter's death: "His death was dreadful. I think he lay on his sick bed about a fortnight. He cried bitterly for mercy—mercy, and told his folks that he was going to hell. He said he couldn't be saved. O, he said, my feet and legs are in hell."

The man's dying words had an effect. "I then made up my mind that I would try to do better," Pearce wrote. "I resolved that I would not swear, or get drunk any more. Here was the first time and place where I think God awakened me to think on the affairs of my soul."

Pearce would relapse into drinking and wickedness—what he meant by the latter he doesn't say—but now those activities gained significance as the lapses of a sinner on his way to salvation.

A Pilgrim's Progress

Pearce may not have been capable of writing his autobiography, but in its telling, he shows himself to be a savvy storyteller. He borrowed elements from the biblical stories of Job, Moses, Daniel and even Jesus Christ in the telling of his own tale:

> *Then he hauled me forward and laid me over the windlass, and made one of the hands hold me over while he laid on three or four hard blows with a rope, and made me promise not to pray again. Then I didn't know what to do. I thought if we got into another storm we should sartinly [sic] be lost; and I knew if I did not pray I should sartinly go to hell. I wept a good deal—pretty much all night long.*
>
> *And then it seemed to me that God wouldn't hear my prayer, if I didn't shut my eyes. Well, what to do I didn't know—but finally I thought I would risk it, and shut my eyes. So I shut my eyes, and glory to God! I don't know whether I was praying or no, but I felt right off delivered from all my 'stress [distress]—and oh, how happy I felt! Seemed as if I felt a great burden roll off of me…I loved every body.*

And, then, the Cecil B. DeMille moment:

> [A]*ll at once the Lord come to me, and says, "Cato, Cato." "Sir." He had a candle-stick, with a candle in it lit, in one hand, and a bible in t' other, and the room was as light as day. He handed me the bible and told me to read. Well, I looked into the bible and I know'd every letter, but couldn't pronounce the words. Says I, "Lord, I can't read." Says he, "Try again." Says I, "Lord, I can't read." He said the third time, "Try again," I says, "Lord, I can't read—I can't pronounce the words." "Well," says he, "follow me—go to my house and I will teach you."*

Pearce followed. He braved murderous soldiers, resisted the temptations of hell, faced down a demon and witnessed a tree bearing beautiful fruit. Pearce's reward? A meeting with God, his wife and his daughter. Go figure.

God told Pearce that his name is written in His Bible—guaranteed salvation. But there's more. God's wife said, "I can give him something that will make him pray or preach or sing." She ladled a drop of something on Pearce's tongue, and the heavens sang. Really. Pearce said, "Sich [*sic*] singin' I never heard; and don't know as I ever 'spect to till I get to heaven."

Pearce was able to preach and to read the Bible. And he was given his mission: "And [God] took his place before me, and his wife and his darter [*sic*] just the same as they stood at first, and stood a minute, and then he laid one hand on my head and the other on my breast, and said, 'Your sins are forgiven—and you must go back and preach my gospel, and tell 'em what I have done for you.'"

When Pearce awoke from his reverie, he told his employer's wife, who told her friends. Pearce spread the word to neighbors. Meetings commenced and souls were saved, Pearce recalled in his autobiography.

Of course, there's always one skeptic in the mix, and this one, Elisha R. Potter of Kingston, saw fit to threaten violence and punish Pearce with jail time.

After his fantastical vision—Pearce called it his "'spearance"—Pearce was baptized and commenced with his preaching career, leading and attending meetings of predominantly white folk. By his account, he was much in demand as an evangelical speaker, but finances required Pearce to work for Potter, a prominent white man from Kingston. Trouble came when Pearce requested and received permission from Potter to attend a meeting. Pearce hired a man to tend to his chores for Potter and left. When he returned the next day, Potter confronted him, horsewhip in hand, and threatened to whip Pearce if he persisted in preaching. But Potter opted to jail his hired hand instead.

This didn't go over well with the neighbors, Pearce recalled:

> *It happened to be in Court time and it "[a]larmed the people and they wanted to know what I was put in prison for, I told 'em for preachin." I staid in there two nights and part of two days. I could say within myself, "Thank God I was willin' to lay my bones there—and I could give God the glory. And I had another comfortable thought—that Elisha Potter had n't* [sic] *got all the power—but God had the power in heaven and earth."*

And Pearce, well, he had a little power, too. Sheriff Allen and other "great men" came to visit Pearce in jail. They gave him money and assured him that he would be released shortly or that Potter would be prosecuted. Potter caved to public pressure and told Pearce through an intermediary that he could go preach every weekend if he wanted to. Pearce didn't allow Potter to be the hero, though. That was Pearce's part.

He told the jailer: "If [Potter] has put me in here, amen—if I have got to stay here and die, amen to it: I have nothin' to do with him about it. I never have stole nor cheated nor done any thing wrong to him. Says I, 'I want you to put me back into my room—I don't want to talk any more about it.'"

Potter asked Pearce to return to his job. Pearce declined. He was released, and the ensuing scene was reminiscent of the one where God's better half gave him the heavenly elixir. Cue the music.

"When I stepped out into the street, my soul was happy," Pearce said. "'Mediately I was surrounded by many friends and brethren. I went singin' through the street, and felt to give God the glory that wa'n't [sic] put in for any thing but preachin."

Pearce would be jailed again. And released again. He would convert many and retire to Cranston, to the home of Dea. [Deacon] Thomas Cole.

That so much should have been accomplished by one born to so little must have been a remarkable thing in 1842, the date of the book's publication. What Pearce could not have known is that his thirty-four-page history is most remarkable for its being "the most complete account by a Rhode Island–born African American who made the transition from slavery to freedom," said Christian M. McBurney, who wrote an introduction to Pearce's autobiography in 2006.

Regardless of whether Pearce's visions were to be believed or not, his was a miraculous life. And the former slave turned preacher knew it. He closed his autobiography saying: "Many other things I want to say, but now I must stop—hopin' God will bless what I have here said to all who may read it. I feel that I'm on my way home and shall soon git there."

McBurney wrote that Pearce lived his remaining days in Rhode Island but did not put a date to his death. What is assured is that the preacher left the world in a better state than when he entered it: he died a free man.

The Murder of Danny Walsh: The Luck of the Irish Runs Out

In the days following Danny Walsh's disappearance, when the police came with their questions, his neighbors made the usual, safe comments: "He kept to himself" and "He minded his own business."

But what did they whisper?

Danny Walsh was a rumrunner, a common criminal. That fancy farm with its prize horses, the apartment on the East Side, the thousands of dollars that routinely lined his pockets? All of it only bought him an early grave.

Danny Walsh lay at the bottom of the sea, his casket a barrel weighted with cement, some claimed. No, no, others argued, Danny Walsh rotted in an unmarked grave on his Charlestown farm. People had spied strange men sprinkling lime to staunch the stench of moldering flesh.

Not that anyone said such things to the police. No one wanted a visit from one of Danny Walsh's "associates."

Danny Walsh disappeared on the evening of February 2, 1933, after dining with a half-dozen men, business associates, at the Bank Café in Pawtuxet Village. He had $40,000 in his pockets. A few days later, Walsh's brother, Joseph, would travel to Boston to pay a $40,000 ransom for the return of his brother. Though the exchange was made, Walsh was not returned. It was an ominous end for the enigmatic Irishman.

Prohibition: "Hell Will Be Forever for Rent"

When the Eighteenth Amendment was passed in January 1919, following a state-level movement to ban alcohol, proponents cheered, believing that they had solved a growing crime problem in America. Supporters of prohibition thought that alcohol was directly linked to a surge in criminal activity unprecedented since the country's founding. Supporters of the amendment tried to appeal to people's better natures. The elimination of alcohol would solve all sorts of social ills, said Reverend Billy Sunday in his famous sermon on the subject: "The reign of tears is over. The slums will soon be a memory. We will turn our prisons into factories and our jails into storehouses and corncribs. Men will walk upright now, women will smile and children will laugh. Hell will be forever for rent."

Sunday must have fancied himself a modern-day John Winthrop for the "City Upon a Hill" flair his own speech had. Of course, Sunday would have done well to remember that Winthrop's utopia didn't exactly pan out. As the Puritans resisted Winthrop's rules, so did society rail against prohibition. Sunday must have been greatly dismayed to see that slums stayed slums. Prisons and jails grew more crowded as criminal activity grew more rampant.

Yes, jobs were created and fortunes made, but in rumrunning and related organized criminal activity. And men may have walked upright—straight backs were better, after all, for hoisting picket signs saying, "We want beer."

And women were smiling, but not in a way that Reverend Sunday would have liked. Frederick Lewis Allen wrote in his *Only Yesterday: An Informal History of the 1920s*:

> *Supposedly nice girls were smoking cigarettes—openly and defiantly, if often rather awkwardly and self-consciously. They*

were drinking—somewhat less openly but often all too efficaciously. There were stories of daughters of the most exemplary parents getting drunk—"blotto"—as their companions cheerfully put it— on the contents of the hip-flasks of the new prohibition regime, and going out joyriding with men at four o'clock in the morning.

As for hell being "forever for rent," prohibition-era parents of teenagers feared that the devil had already taken them:

[I]nnumerable families were torn with dissension over cigarettes and gin and all-night automobile rides. Fathers and mothers lay awake asking themselves whether their children were not utterly lost; sons and daughters evaded questions, lied miserably and unhappily, or flared up to reply rudely that at least they were not dirty-mouthed hypocrites.

The devil, the Bible teaches us, can take many forms—like that of a gentleman farmer fond of racehorses and fast money.

Rhode Island: The "Most Anti-Prohibition State in the Union"

A *Providence Journal* article titled "In the Roaring Twenties the Question Here Was: What Prohibition?" casts Danny Walsh as a big-time Rhode Island bootlegger. Rhode Island was one of two states that did not ratify the Eighteenth Amendment. The unnamed reporter wrote, "If ever there was a state that gleefully thumbed its nose at Prohibition, it was Rhode Island. Throughout the Roaring Twenties, Rhode Island was probably the most anti-prohibition state in the union."

Law enforcement officials were thwarted by four hundred miles of Rhode Island coastline and a criminal enterprise so successful that Al Capone was rumored to have come to Rhode Island to do business. What drew a man like Danny Walsh to associate with men like Al Capone? Money.

Born about 1893, Danny Walsh was a poor kid from the Cumberland village of Valley Falls. Bootlegging offered a life otherwise out of reach. "A bootlegger who ducked arrest couldn't help but get rich," the *Journal* article noted. "Quality alcohol, for instance, was selling wholesale in

Rhode Island in the mid-1920s for $7 a gallon. That same gallon cost 66 cents in Canada, which never adopted Prohibition."

Walsh had a ready customer base in the state's many illegal speakeasies. When in 1928 the Internal Revenue Service sued him for unpaid taxes, Walsh could say that he had arrived. The federal government said that he owed $300,000, which meant he must have earned more than $750,000, the *Journal* reported. He kept not one but two Providence apartments and owned the horse farm in Charlestown. Of the latter, there is a story that Walsh built the house on the borderline between Matunuck and Charlestown. Why? So that when local authorities came for him, Walsh could avoid arrest by retiring to that part of the house that was outside of their jurisdiction.

Walsh's cleverness would appear to have failed him, however. While his murder has never been solved, the *Journal* article reported that strange and potentially revelatory things had been noted on the Charlestown farm in the months after Walsh vanished: "Years after his disappearance, a discovery cast new light on the company Walsh kept. Between September and December 1932, four of Walsh's associates went to the farm and dug a deep grave near an abandoned building. A white powder was dumped into the grave." Several of Walsh's farm employees saw the grave and assumed that the powder was quick lime, used to camouflage the odor of a rotting corpse.

An associate testifying before a federal court talked of Walsh receiving six-figure payoffs and meeting with major organized crime figures. Seems like Walsh met up with the wrong fellas on that fateful night in February. It's pretty safe to assume that Walsh's associates weren't laying down fertilizer.

THE ROOT THAT ATE ROGER WILLIAMS AND OTHER TALES OF OUR FOUNDING FATHER

As career setbacks go, Roger Williams's expulsion from the Massachusetts Bay Colony in the fall of 1635 would seem to be a biggie. There were the pragmatic issues associated with being jobless and homeless in colonial America—namely that if you didn't have shelter

Postcard of the Casino at Roger Williams Park, Providence. *Author's collection.*

Postcard of Betsey Williams's house in Roger Williams Park, Providence. *Author's collection.*

and food before winter set in, you wouldn't likely see the spring. And even if you were fortunate enough to find said shelter and food, it was tough work finding employment in the area of Christian ministry when there weren't any congregations outside of the old neighborhood.

Lesser souls might have despaired. For Williams, though, banishment from the Massachusetts Bay Colony was the career catalyst that spurred the Puritan minister to found a new colony, become its governor, establish the first Baptist church in America, write one of the seminal texts on Native American languages and spread the idea of religious tolerance—a concept that would become one of America's most cherished tenets.

To church authorities, Roger Williams was not the "let there be peace on earth and let it begin with me" type. He was a rabble-rouser and an insurrectionist. At twenty-seven, Williams fled his homeland of England because he was spouting off ideas about breaking with the church and freedom of worship. Unlike other Puritan ministers, who held that it was "Satan's policy to plead for an indefinite and boundless toleration," Williams believed that "to molest any person, Jew or Gentile, for either professing doctrine or practicing worship is to persecute him."

"Uhm, yeah. So?" would have been England's likely response to that impassioned bit. After all, this was England, the country that burned Joan of Arc, beheaded Anne Boleyn and had William Wallace drawn, quartered and castrated before executing him. Enemies to the Crown or the Church—one in the same, really—were not going to be tolerated anywhere.

When Williams got to Massachusetts, he does the same damn thing, and predictably, so do the colony's authorities. According to 1635 court records, Williams was tried and convicted of advancing four "newe and dangerous opinions":

- *That we have not our land by patent from the King, but that the natives are the true owners of it, and that we ought to repent of such a receiving of it by patent.*
- *That it is not lawful to call a wicked person to swear, to pray, as being actions of God's worship.*
- *That it is not lawful to hear any of the ministers of the parish assemblies in England.*
- *That the civil magistrate's power extends only to the bodies and goods, and outward state of men.*

Essentially, Williams believed that the Puritans had no claim to the land, that heretics should be left alone (God would punish them later) and that the Church of England was not to be obeyed.

Fine, said Williams's Puritan neighbors, then pack up and take that Satan talk elsewhere. So Williams headed south to Seekonk. Upon learning, though, that this was still Massachusetts Bay Colony land, he crossed the Seekonk River and arrived in what would become Providence. There Williams ran into some friendly natives, one of whom, legend says, greeted him with the salutation, "What cheer, Netop?" which more or less means, "How's it going, buddy?" In his 1643 *A Key Into the Language of America*, Williams praises his new friends' generosity:

> *If any stranger come in, they presently give him to eate of what they have; many a time, and at all times of the night (as I have fallen in travel upon their houses) when nothing hath been ready, have themselves and their wives, risen to prepare me some refreshing…It is a strange truth, that a man shall generally finde more free entertainment and refreshment among these Barbarians, then amongst thousands that call themselves Christians.*

Williams was speaking of the Narragansetts, who demonstrably shared his live-and-let-live sensibility and sold him the land that he would call Providence. Over the next forty-eight years, Williams lived peaceably with the Narragansetts, as well as the Jews and Gentiles who came to reside in the Ocean State. Williams did see his beloved Providence burn during King Philip's War, fought in 1675 and 1676. But he remained consistent in his message of tolerance until his death.

Weird Rhode Island fact: its heroes' remains have a tendency to be unearthed and reburied: Roger Williams, thrice; Nathanael Greene, twice; and Oliver Hazard Perry, thrice.

Roger Williams died in 1683 or 1684, likely at the age of eighty, and was first buried on his property, which became the site of the Sullivan Dorr mansion on the corner of Benefit and Bowen Streets. In 1860, a descendant of Roger Williams succeeded in his quest to retrieve Williams's remains from the site for reburial in Providence's North Burial Ground.

Not surprisingly, the disinterment of the 177-year-old corpse yielded only a few bone fragments. It was what lay with those fragments that, well, weirded people out and secured Williams's place in the state's supernatural lore.

It bears mention here that Roger Williams's championing of religious tolerance had an effect on the burial practices of the people of Rhode Island. Early colonial graveyards were usually affiliated with churches in towns in which everybody pretty much agreed when it came to matters of religion. Early Rhode Islanders, being diverse in their religious affiliations and practices, opted for backyard burials. This occasionally had gruesome ramifications, noted Howard M. Chapin in his 1918 *Report Upon the Burial Place of Roger Williams*: "Near Bowen street, whilst cultivating a garden, Nicholas Esten pulled up the fragments of a human skull, attached to the roots of a cabbage." Bury grandma in the backyard and you just might be serving her up for dinner one night in the future.

Roger Williams was buried in an apple orchard. At the disinterment, Chapin wrote, witnesses found that a

> *tree had pushed downwards one of its main roots in a sloping direction and nearly straight course toward the precise spot that had been occupied by the skull of Roger Williams. There making a turn conforming with its circumference, the root followed the direction of the backbone to the hips, and thence divided into two branches, each one following a leg bone to the heel, where they both turned upwards to the extremities of the toes of the skeleton. One of the roots formed a slight crook at the part occupied by the knee joint, thus producing an increased resemblance to the outlines of the skeleton of Roger Williams, as if indeed, moulded there by the powers of vegetable life.*

Chapin then added a *Little Shop of Horrors* touch, bestowing predatory powers to the tree root: "Apparently not stated [sated] with banqueting on the remains found in one grave, the same roots extended themselves into the next adjoining one, pervading every part of it with a network of voracious fibres in their thorough search for every particle of nutritious matter."

Eew.

The Rhode Island Historical Society's official position is that "the story of the Roger Williams Root remains one of the great Rhode Island myths, a blend of fact and fiction that has further perpetuated the legend of the founder of Rhode Island." But the historical society did keep the root and label it "Apple Tree Root Taken From the Grave of Roger Williams."

There is no extant painting or drawing of Roger Williams; his face will always be a mystery. But how many states can claim to have a root in their founder's likeness? Not many, I bet.

Roger Williams's root resides in the Rhode Island Historical Society's collection at the John Brown House Museum on Power Street, in Providence. Roger Williams's remains were relocated once again in 1936, on the 300th anniversary of the founding of Providence. The founder's likely permanent, almost certainly final, this-time-it's-for-real resting place is beneath a statue in his likeness at Prospect Terrace.

There are even more weird footnotes to the Roger Williams story. Some are as wild as the bone-sucking rogue root—like Williams's rebel-with-a-divine-cause story becoming the subject of a *New York Times* bestseller in 2008.

Sarah Vowell—*This American Life* contributor, *New York Times* bestselling author and voice of Violet in Pixar's *The Incredibles*—rendered Roger Williams cool, if crazy, in her bestseller *The Wordy Shipmates*. She made appearances on both *Late Night with David Letterman* and *The Daily Show with Jon Stewart*. But Vowell seems far less star struck with television legends than with the shades of Winthrop and Williams. Of the latter, she wrote admiringly:

> *It's one thing for nonviolent nonbelievers to throw up their hands at the way the faithful of various religious faiths seem to come to blows over dogma. But Williams, a diehard zealot, is unflinching in his recognition that other diehard zealots are equally set in their ways. And while he would happily—happily—harangue any other persons of faith for days on end about how wrong they are, he does not think they should be jailed or hit or stabbed or shot for their stupidity, the eternal flames of hell being punishment enough.*

If only everyone could content themselves with others' assured eternal damnation, peace on earth could be a real possibility.

Rhode Island has paid tribute to its founder; a national park (Roger Williams Park Zoo), a medical facility (Roger Williams Medical Center) and a university (Roger Williams University) bear his name. Rhode Island boasts three of five known statues of Roger Williams (the farthest flung is in Geneva, Switzerland, at the Monument to the Heroes of the Reformation, according to the National Park Service's website). As mentioned earlier, there's no known likeness of Roger Williams in existence, no extant painting to aid artists in the sculpting of Rhode Island's founder, leaving them to improvise as they chose. At least one of those artists was a baseball fan with a sense of humor. The statue at Roger Williams University bears the visage of Red Sox legend Ted Williams.

There is also a monument in Slate Rock Park that commemorates Williams's arrival in Rhode Island. Apparently, Williams alighted on a slate ledge after crossing the Seekonk. Unfortunately, when the state built Gano Street in 1828, it did so by dumping a lot of fill into the Seekonk River. So the monument isn't on the water. And there's no rock, either. In 1877, city workers trying to unearth more of the rock to preserve it for posterity accidentally blew it up.

But Williams's name will not be forgotten. In fact, it has been used to sell everything from baby onesies and beer to used cars. A few favorites follow.

Baby apparel: Called "infant creepers" (a creepy name), these tiny T-shirts are emblazoned with big tributes, such as, "February 5: Roger Williams, defender of religious liberty, advocate for fair dealings with Native Americans, founder of Rhode Island, arrived in Boston on the Lyon from England today in 1631" and, "Born on August 20, Roger Williams pledged in Rhode Island today in 1636 the majority would leave the liberty of conscience to the individual." The shirts are offered by shop.cafepress.com at fifteen dollars each. Certainly in such a shirt your baby will look far smarter than the kid wearing "Got Milk?" or "Gramma Loves Me."

Beer: The now defunct Roger Williams Brewing Corporation offered Roger Williams Ale in cans depicting the state's founder, in red cape, weird cap and Dutch boy hair, holding a bottle of brew backlit by the rays of the setting sun. At the time of the writing of this piece, the website taverntrove.com offered a 1937 Roger Williams Brewing Company bottle cap for the bargain price of $38.49. It turns out that it's not that far-fetched that Williams would have been a beer fan. Massachusetts author Andy Crouch wrote in his 2006 book *The Good Beer Guide to New England* that Rhode Island was home to one of the first American breweries thanks to you know who: "In 1639, Roger Williams placed a communal brew house and tavern under the supervision of Sergeant Baulston in Providence."

Dollhouses: Providence-based Roger Williams Toys battled Germany (number-one dollhouse maker) for supremacy in the U.S. markets during World War II. And paper doll likenesses of Roger Williams occasionally turn up on the web. It doesn't appear that Mattel ever released a Barbie version of Roger Williams, though.

Burgers: The Hotel Roger Williams in New York City offers the Roger Williams Cheeseburger for sixteen dollars. According to the hotel menu, that gets you "ground sirloin, edam cheese and baked fries."

Part III
Rogues

JAMES GORDON BENNETT JR.: NEWPORT'S MOST NOTORIOUS NAKED BAD BOY

New York Herald publishing heir James Gordon Bennett Jr. set the bar for spectacularly bad behavior.

On New Year's Day 1877, Bennett attended a house party at the home of his future in-laws. At that time, it was the tradition among members of New York society to travel from house to house, enjoying eggnog and wishing one another well in the new year. Nice tradition, in theory.

Bennett arrived late to the home of his fiancée, Caroline May. He was also quite drunk upon arrival. One version of the story holds that Bennett arrived drunk and late to what was his engagement party to the New York socialite. Some heated discussion must have ensued because what Bennett did next could not have been unprovoked.

Bennett dropped his pants and urinated in full view of guests into the family's drawing room fireplace. Some witnesses later said that he'd meant to hit the grand piano but that his aim was off. So, as it turned out, was his engagement. Caroline fainted. Bennett was thrown out. Caroline's brother accosted Bennett several days later with a horsewhip, and the whole incident was included in that year's *Guinness Book of World Records* under the heading of "worst engagement faux pas," according to Larry Standford's book *Wicked Newport: Sordid Stories from the City by the Sea*.

Surprisingly, a reputation for exposing oneself and public urination in a private home did not cure Bennett of his outrageous behavior. Public nudity was something of a habit for him. A favorite activity after a night of drinking was to drive his horse-drawn coach full speed down Newport streets naked. Another inexplicable habit of Bennett's was to announce his arrival at New York restaurants by yanking the tablecloths off other diners' tables while they were in the middle of enjoying dinner. Bennett would pay for the interruption and damages caused.

His most costly prank, though, occurred in Newport in 1878. Bennett had introduced the sport of polo to both New York and Newport. Among his polo friends was Captain Henry Augustus "Sugar" Candy, an Englishman. Bennett dared Candy to ride his polo pony onto the front porch and into the lobby of the Reading Room on tony Bellevue Avenue. Candy was more than game and charged the club, rearing the horse up onto its hind legs for high dramatic effect. The members were not amused and yelled, "Get down off your high horse," Stanford wrote.

Now, a word about the Reading Room: This was a hardcore men's club. No women were allowed. Little reading was done. Smoking, cursing and drinking were the favored pastimes. It is said that self-respecting women didn't even want to walk by the club for fear of ungentlemanly remarks being directed their way.

So, given the Reading Room's locker room milieu, it seems a little shrewish for the members to have rescinded Candy's guest pass and rebuked Bennett after Candy charged the porch. Bennett didn't take the criticism very well.

Watch young children in a sandbox, and you'll see play that has hard-and-fast rules. Dominance is established and alliances are formed. And if you can't play by the rules, then you have to leave the sandbox. Bennett was like the kid who would stomp the sandcastle everyone else was working on.

It's amazing, really, that a man of such unbridled behavior as Bennett would adhere to anyone else's rules for very long. After being chastised by the members of the Reading Room, Bennett did exactly what any five-year-old with ample disposable income would do: he founded his own club. In 1881, Bennett hired Stanford White—a notorious partier, womanizer and member of the esteemed architectural firm McKim, Mead & White—to design and oversee the building of the Newport Casino. The casino became the summer hot spot for Newport's elite and common folk, as well.

And that's how you pick up your shovel and leave the sandbox in high style.

THE SHORT, SAD LIFE OF AARON CHURCH, WOULD-BE SCOURGE OF THE SEVEN SEAS

Aaron Church wanted off Block Island.

The endless ocean views, the breathtaking bluffs, the grassy vistas, the sheer unadulterated beauty of it—it was all driving him nuts. Church wanted to see the world beyond the ten miles of Manisses, the

Postcard of the Mohegan Bluffs, Block Island. *Author's collection.*

Narragansett name for the island. Church wanted to rove with the winds and go where the tides would take him. He wanted something different, specifically "the wild, roistering life of rough companions in mainland ports and promise of easy gold," wrote Ethel Colt Ritchie in *Block Island Lore and Legends*. Church wanted to be a pirate.

So when the opportunity came to escape on one of the many sloops that visited Block Island, Church left. In 1830, he found himself in the crew of the *Vinyard*, a brig bearing molasses, sugar and $54,000 belonging to Philadelphia banker Stephen Girard. Church and two crewmates, Charles Gibbs and Thomas J. Wansley, wanted the ship and its stores for themselves and so led a mutiny. According to Ritchie, they murdered their captain and first mate and tossed their bodies into the sea. Gibbs then took command and set a course for Long Island. Fifteen miles off its shores, the three murderous coconspirators divided the loot and destroyed the ship.

The trio then parted ways. Gibbs and Wansley took a long boat and, with some of the crew, headed for the Long Island shoreline. Church and a few other crew members set a course for Block Island, some fourteen miles distant. Church's boat capsized in the vicinity of Mohegan Bluffs. Witnesses said that Gibbs and Wansley were still near enough to see Church and crew struggle to survive. Gibbs and Wansley watched their shipmates drown, unmoved even as the hapless sailors clawed mast and rigging in a desperate attempt to save themselves. "Such was the end of an Island lad who had gone to seek fortune on the high seas and it is perhaps fitting that he found his grave near the shores of his birthplace," Ritchie says. Church would likely have found this a small consolation.

He had hoped, no doubt, to return to New Shoreham as the infamous pirate Aaron Church. A hero's welcome certainly would not have awaited him, but Church may have settled for being loathed rather than loved. Infamy had its advantages. Instead, though, Church's would be another cautionary tale: a misguided boy falls victim to greed and pays for his sins with his life—a story so familiar as to be ordinary, even dull. No songs would be sung, no hair-raising stories told of the exploits of Aaron Church. His was a tale some hoped would soon be forgotten.

View of Block Island. *Photo by author.*

Church's own father, in fact, was happy to hear of his dissolute son's demise, saying, "I have always been sorry that Aaron became a pirate. I am glad his career is ended."

CHARLES HARRIS: A TRUE PIRATE GETS HIS BUT GOOD

In the golden age of piracy, the waters off the coast of Rhode Island teemed with profligates happy to relieve ships of their cargo and crew. This was a singular class of villains, alternately reviled and romanticized. Even the most murderous landlubber's boasts were no match for the whispered tales of mayhem committed by the likes of Blackbeard, Captain Kidd and Calico Jack.

Charles Harris's career as a pirate was brief, just eighteen months, but he won his place in maritime history by apprenticing himself to two of the most fearsome pirates to plague the Atlantic: Edward Low and George Lowther. They were impressed with young Harris, giving the twenty-four-year-old his own sloop within ten days of his signing Lowther's articles of piracy. Eighteen months later, though, the promising lad, along with twenty-five of his crew, would swing from the gallows at Gravelly Point in Newport.

The London-born Harris started as a respectable seafarer, first mate on the Boston ship *Greyhound*. In early January 1722, the ship was captured by Captain George Lowther's vessel *Happy Delivery*. This was no joyful encounter for the *Greyhound*, though, whose cargo (timber) was a disappointment to the pirates. They took it out on the *Greyhound*'s commander, Benjamin Edwards, and his crew, lashing their shoulders and backs with cutlasses, wrote George Francis Dow and John Henry Edmonds in *The Pirates of the New England Coast, 1630–1730*: "By way of diversion two of the unoffending sailors were triced [*sic*] up at the foot of the mainmast and lashed until the blood ran from their backs. Captain Edwards and his men were then ordered into the boats and sent on board the pirate ship and the 'Greyhound' was set on fire."

When Edwards and his men boarded the *Happy Delivery*, they were greeted with a mug of rum and an invitation to join the pirate crew. This was somewhat perfunctory on the part of the pirates, as the sailors were often compelled to join if they did not volunteer. Harris signed Lowther's articles in days, and within a month of his capture Lowther had given Harris the command of a captured sloop. In May, Harris abandoned the sloop and signed on with Low, who had been given command of a one-hundred-ton Rhode Island sloop captured by Lowther.

If Lowther was a demon, Low was the devil. English by birth, Low, who hailed from Boston, liked to brutalize French and Portuguese seafarers. He favored cutting the lips, ears and/or noses off his foreign captives, sometimes forcing his victims to eat their own flesh. In May 1722, Low gave Harris a captured schooner called *Fancy* but relieved Harris of his command shortly after. Whatever falling out the two may have had did not result in Harris's disfigurement and appeared to be resolved five months later when Harris was again sailing with Low.

In early May 1723, the pair captured the *Amsterdam Merchant*, and Low, in a spiteful move, sliced the right ear off the ship's captain, John Welland of Boston. After looting the *Amsterdam Merchant*, Low and Harris sunk it. Welland survived and was put on another vessel that happened by, after Harris and Low had pillaged that one, too. Welland and his men sailed to Portsmouth without further incident. If Harris had the gift of foresight, he likely would have killed Welland, as it was the maimed captain's testimony that would be most damaging in Harris's later trial.

A Pirate's Life Cut Short

Just a month later, Harris's short stint as a pirate captain would be over. On June 10, 1723, he and Low, steering eastward in the waters off Long Island, caught sight of a man-of-war, the HMS *Grayhound*, captained by Peter Solgard. They gave chase but soon found themselves the pursued. In *Pirates*, Dow and Edmonds reprint a June 20, 1723 account of what ensued that had been published in the *Boston News-Letter*.

According to the account, Solgard brought into Newport a crew of forty-eight, along with a well-provisioned sloop outfitted with eight guns. While Low evaded capture, the apprehension of Harris's sloop was a big win for Solgard. It was the biggest pirate bust the colonies had ever seen. What follows is a sailor's eyewitness account of the events, with spelling errors and odd capitalization intact:

> *The Fire continued on both sides for about an hour; but when the hall'd from us with the help of their Oars, we left off Firing, and turned to Rowing with 86 Hands, and half an Hour past Two in the afternoon we came up with them; when they clapt on a Wind to receive us; we again kept close to Windward, and ply'd them warmly with small and grape shot; and during the Action we fell between them, having shot down one of their Main Sails we kept close to him and at 4 a Clock he call'd for Quarters; at 5 having got the Prisoners on board, we continued to Chase the other Sloop, when at 8 a Clock in the Evening he bore from us N.W. by W. two Leagues, when we lost sight [sight] of him near Block Island.*

It was a bitter battle, with casualties: eight wounded and four killed—one pirate by his own hand. According to the *News-Letter*, "One

Desperado was for blowing up this Sloop rather than surrendering, and being hindered, he went forward, and with his Pistol shot out his own Brains."

The crew of the HMS *Grayhound*—ironically the man-of-war bore the same name as the vessel upon which Harris had last done an honest day's work—were also disappointed with the outcome of the battle. Solgard and his men believed that they had wounded many of Low's men, critically damaged his ship and would have taken both vessels if they'd had more time.

Harris and his men were taken to the gaol in Newport, where they awaited trial. Justice would be swift and severe. The court of admiralty brought the pirates to trial on July 10, exactly one month after Harris's run-in with Solgard.

The pirates' defense was a common one: they had been forced into the life. Almost all maintained that Low had virtually kidnapped them and forced them, upon threat of death, to serve as his henchmen. Many insisted, too, that they, unlike Harris, had never signed the articles, a pirate's de facto employment contract, nor shared in any of the plunder from the capture of other vessels.

The pirates' "Captain Low made me do it" arguments were a waste of words. The advocate general decried:

> *Their malicious and cruel assault upon Capt. Welland, not only in the spoiling of his goods, but what is much more, the cutting off his right ear, a crime of that nature and barbarity which can neer ben repaired: Their plea of constraint, or force, (in the mouth of every Pirate) can be of no avail to them, for if that could justify or excuse!*

Twenty-six were sentenced to be hanged at Gravelly Point, Newport, on July 19. Their sentence was carried out between the hours of 12:00 p.m. and 1:00 p.m. before an assembly that came by foot and by boat to watch the spectacle of so many executed at once. The pirates' bodies were buried on Goat and Fort Islands. No doubt some of those who died that day were bona fide pirates—violent, lawless plunderers willingly corrupted by the promise of easy riches and easier women. And there likely were others who were truly forced, threatened with death if they did not submit. Some maintained their innocence to the very end; others made public professions of contrition.

But all swung.

CAPTAIN WILLIAM KIDD:
COME FOR HIS GOLD AND HE'LL COME FOR YOU

Captain William Kidd needed hanging not once but twice before he expired.

Convicted of piracy and murder, Kidd, once a revered privateer in the service of the English King William III, died at Execution Dock, London, during low tide on the afternoon of May 23, 1701. One account of the execution, Willard Hallam Bonner's "The Ballad of Captain Kidd," sets the scene: "The crowd made holiday, howling, laughing, quarreling, swilling beer and gin, hurling impudent and ribald jests, picking pockets,

Captain Kidd is said to have buried treasure on Block Island. *Photo by author.*

Illustration of a Pirate Ghost, artist Howard Pyle.

hawking wares, elbowing for the wall, singing ballads, reading broadsides, eluding or engaging strolling whores—one continual fair all the way."

He could have been describing Woodstock or a Renaissance fair or Times Square, but Bonner casts Kidd's execution as theater. It was as an all-out raucous party, and the guest of honor was, Bonner says, "more often than not drunk or drinking hard, uttering vilification and blasphemy that might turn, however, to moral speech and dying confession upon the scaffold."

To expect sobriety and manners of a man headed for the noose hardly seems appropriate. This was William Kidd, after all, one of the most dangerous men ever to raise sails. Or was he? Evidence discovered long after Kidd's death suggests that he was innocent—at least of charges of piracy.

After death, Kidd's body was chained and gibbeted, meaning bound in iron bands, a plunderer's flesh left to the predations of nature. For two years, the putrid, caged remains of the convicted murderer and presumed pirate hung in what was a very public warning to those who might mistakenly romanticize a pirate's life. Kidd's remains twisting in the wind were testament to the fact that this kind of error could prove fatal.

It is difficult to mine Kidd's legend for fact. Even his birth date is in dispute. Some scholars set the date of his birth at 1645 and others at 1655. All accounts agree that his place of birth was Scotland. According to George Francis Dow and John Henry Edmonds's book, *Pirates of the New England Coast 1630–1730*, Kidd was likely the child of "Rev. John Kidd who suffered the torture of the boot." That could mean that his feet were either lathered with lard and roasted, immobilized and boiled or that they were placed in viselike instruments and crushed.

Some say that the family lost their livelihood when Kidd's father died; as soon as he was old enough, Kidd chose to go to sea. Dow and Edmonds wrote that Kidd was in command of a privateer in August 1689. In 1691, Kidd's crew mutinied and took his ship while he was ashore. In May of that same year, Kidd suffered another blow to his reputation when he lost a French ship due to his lackadaisical pursuit, or so his detractors said to the governor of New York. Still, five years later, Richard Coote—Earl of Bellomont and governor of the Provinces of New York, Massachusetts and New Hampshire—obtained from King

Captain Kidd in New York Harbor, artist Jean Leon Gerome Ferris.

Kidd on the Deck of the Adventure Galley, artist Howard Pyle.

William III a commission for Kidd to apprehend pirates and strip them of their ill-gotten bounty. Altogether, Kidd received £6,000 from various nobles to purchase and refit the *Adventure Galley*. In turn, Kidd was to take pirates and their plunder to Boston and deliver them to Bellomont. The king was to receive one-tenth of everything captured and the crew one-fourth of the remainder. Kidd and his partner, Robert Livingston, were to share in one-fifth of whatever bounty remained, provided the total taken was worth £100,000 or more. Moreover, Kidd would be given the *Adventure Galley* for his troubles.

Kidd's commission went beyond the usual "plunder all foreign enemies and especially the French" edicts. England's King William III wanted

Kidd to apprehend Newport pirate Thomas Tew, among others. Kidd agreed to the terms and set sail for the Indian Ocean from New York on September 5, 1696. Two years later, Kidd learned that, like Tew, he was among the hunted as well.

Murder and Mayhem

It was a tough voyage. An outbreak of cholera took one-third of Kidd's crew. The new ship sprung leaks. There were stories that Kidd failed more than once to apprehend enemy vessels. And mutiny was a constant threat.

Hostilities reached a head when Kidd killed his gunner, William Moore, by fracturing his skull with an iron-bound bucket. He would later claim that Moore was mutinous. But there were other tales of cruelty, of prisoners being hung by their arms and beaten with cutlasses. Some scholars argue that Kidd's crew did this without his permission; he had to take hardened criminals as replacements for crew members who had died due to cholera or had been conscripted by the Royal Navy. It's possible that such men acted independently.

The most damning evidence against Kidd was the charge that he had turned pirate after capturing the *Quedagh Merchant*, a vessel captained by an Englishman under French protection. Kidd wanted to leave the ship and its crew alone. Its captain was an Englishman, after all. But his crew did not agree. The ship was loaded with valuables like gold, silver and silk, and Kidd's crew wanted it all. Kidd acquiesced and unwittingly set a course for his death. In the West Indies, he learned that he had been proclaimed a pirate.

Through correspondence with Bellomont, Kidd agreed to meet two of the earl's men off the coast of Block Island to state his case. Kidd argued that he did nothing to violate his commission. The men related this to Bellomont, who subsequently wrote a letter to Kidd promising him that he would secure a pardon: "I assure you on my Word and Honour I will perform nicely what I have promised through this I declare beforehand that whatever goods and treasure you may bring hither, I will not meddle with the least bit of them; but they shall be left with such persons as the Council shall advise until I receive orders from England how they shall be disposed of."

Kidd agreed to head to Boston, but he did so by a circuitous route. He visited Gardiner Island, off the coast of Long Island, where, legend has it, he left a chest and a box of gold dust, among other goods. Such actions suggest that Kidd mistrusted the earl, but after his wife, Sarah Oort, and their two girls, Elizabeth and Sarah, joined him, the family sailed to Boston. They arrived in Boston Harbor on Saturday, July 1. Kidd and his men faced three days of questioning by authorities, and the captain promised a full report of his activities in writing. But the earl had not been honest. On July 6, Bellomont told those involved that he had orders to arrest Kidd, and the pirate was apprehended in the governor's own house. Dow and Edmonds wrote: "At first Kidd was confined in the house of the prison keeper, but after a day or two he was ordered placed in the stone gaol and kept in irons. His lodgings were searched and in two sea beds were found gold dust and ingots to the value of about 1000 [pounds] and a bag of silver containing money and pigs of silver."

Kidd spent seven months to the day in the Boston jail before being transported to England to await trial before the London High Court of Admiralty.

The earl admitted his betrayal in a December 6, 1701 letter reprinted by Dow and Edmonds: "I own I wrote to Kidd to come to New York after I knew he had turned pirate. Menacing him would not bring him but rather wheedling and that way I took and after that manner got him to Boston and secured him." (Clearly Bellomont was a man familiar with the concept of political correctness. And "wheedling"? Ninny.) Had Kidd known and been able, he would no doubt have found use for another multipurpose, iron-bound bucket.

Kidd was sent to England to await trial.

The Trial and Tribulations of a Murderous Rogue

Kidd faced multiple charges of piracy and one of murder. He had no legal representation at his trials. The first was for the murder of William Moore. Kidd did not deny having killed his mate but argued that it was a necessary evil to prevent a mutiny. Not so, said Kidd's prosecutors, arguing that he was not justified but rather was "moved and seduced by the instigations of the Devil," Dow and Edmonds quote. Kidd was found guilty of murder.

On the charges of piracy that formed the basis of the second trial, Kidd proclaimed his innocence. Kidd argued that exonerating evidence existed in the form of French documents that he had confiscated and given to Bellomont for safekeeping. Big mistake. Bellomont said that he had sent them to authorities in England. And there they got lost.

To say that this was bad news was an understatement. Kidd, now a convicted murderer, couldn't produce the passes and so had no defense. He was sentenced to death by hanging.

On May 23, 1701, Captain William Kidd was hanged not once but twice at Execution Dock, Wapping, in London. The rope broke the first time. This detail, and countless others real and imagined, would serve to ensure Kidd's place in infamy and inspire poets, authors and even moviemakers hundreds of years after his death.

The Making of a Legend

In eighteenth-century England, crimes like Kidd's didn't just sell papers. There was money to be made in music, too. Thus the murderous Kidd became the subject of ballads, the pop songs of the day. A few copies still exist, preserved in the hallowed libraries of Brown and Harvard Universities. Oftentimes these ballads were curious mixes of confession and contrition, at once salacious and pious, in an "I found God in the eleventh hour" kind of way.

One ditty, called "Captain Kid's Farewell to the Seas, or, the Famous Pirate's Lament, 1701," casts Kidd as an unrepentant murderer:

> *Many long leagues from shore when I sail'd, (when I sail'd),*
> *Many long leagues from shore when I sail'd,*
> *Many long leagues from shore*
> *I murdered William Moore,*
> *And laid him in his gore, when I sail'd.*

Because a word he spoke when I sail'd, (when I sail'd)
Because a word he spoke when I sail'd,
Because a word he spoke,
I with a bucket broke
His scull at one sad stroke, when I sail'd.

Catchy.

Ballads were printed and sold at public executions, like playbills. Also, famous criminals like Kidd were put on display while awaiting trial. People paid viewing fees to see the accused caged like zoo attractions. What would Kidd think to know that people would continue to pay, much later, to see movies like 1945's *Captain Kidd* and 1954's *Captain Kidd and the Slave Girl. Peter Pan* author J.M. Barrie paid his respects by placing Captain Hook's pirate ship in Kidd's Creek, and Edgar Allan Poe's "The Gold Bug" also owes a debt to Kidd. The singing produce of *VeggieTales* mention Kidd in their sea shanty "The Pirates Who Don't Do Anything." And the *Pirates of the Caribbean* movies appropriate a fair number of motifs that could be ascribed to Kidd's legend. The movies' creators had better be careful, though. Kidd has ways of dealing with those who would try to take from him.

A Pirate's Postscript

There are some who say that Captain Kidd and his crew still prowl the Atlantic. If they are to be believed, the takeaway is that Kidd is not about to relinquish his booty to a bunch of tropical shirt–sporting, metal detector–wielding amateur treasure hunters. In the absence of a corporeal form with which to dispatch the thieving landlubbers, Kidd resorts to the next best thing: he scares them silly.

A *New York Times* article dated October 19, 1884, quoted a lifelong Block Islander, Mrs. Rose, recounting her uncle's nearly successful attempt to plunder the famed pirate. Said uncle and some other aspiring fortune hunters went to Sandy Point in hopes of unearthing a pot of gold that Kidd had allegedly buried there. It's interesting to note here that oftentimes pirates allegedly buried not treasure chests but pots of gold. Storytellers possibly mixed motifs, swapping treasure chests for cauldrons and pirates for leprechauns. Or it could be that Kidd was a leprechaun. But that's unlikely. He was Scottish, after all.

So, one late fall evening, brightened by a full moon, the island fortune hunters set out. In addition to the usual treasure hunting paraphernalia—pickaxes and shovels—this industrious group also carried with it a diving rod. This was a special diving rod, evidently, that detected not water but buried treasure. The diving rod did its work, and the group set to digging silently. It was a rule that no one could speak until the pot was unearthed. After fifteen minutes of digging, spade struck metal.

Mrs. Rose, in remarkably precise detail, recounts to the *New York Times* what happened next: "With redoubled zeal the moneydiggers fell to work, and a few thrusts of the spade disclosed a large, rusted, iron pot solidly wedged into the hard soil. With half-smothered exclamations, the men dropped on their knees, and, digging the earth away from the rim with their fingers, strained every muscle to lift the treasure from its resting place."

The pot proved very heavy, but the men managed to hoist it within an inch or two of the ground, Mrs. Rose said. But they were stopped by a low cry from one man standing watch. They look in the man's direction and, to their horror, see

> *an apparition advancing from the ocean. It was of a large ship's boat, manned with armed sailors, whose glistening oars as it glided easily through the surf waves rose and fell with the rhythmic swing of practiced oarsmanship. The crew were a ghostly one, in conical peak hats, with shining buckles and trappings, and carrying long-barreled flint locks. In the bow was a figure with drawn sword, unmistakably that of the pirate Captain Kidd.*

This is a remarkable identification to make by moonlight from shore, to be sure.

Mrs. Rose continued: "What most astonished the spell-bound group was that the boat and its occupants seemed to be of gray, impalpable mist, like one of the erratic ocean vapors that suddenly and at unexpected times sweep down the island and trail their cold, filmy swathes along the valleys and headlands."

And those cold, filmy vapors were headed right for the treasure seekers:

The phantom boat swept over the tumbling surf waves to the strand, the crew leaped on the shore, and in an instant a gray-white mist rushed up the slope, enveloping the hill and the money diggers. There was a vivid flash of lightning, followed by a peal of thunder. The affrighted gold seekers hesitated no longer. They dropped their tools, and without turning a backward glance, fled through the wet sea grass, not pausing until they were a quarter of a mile from the hill.

When the "money diggers" got to what they thought was far enough away, they turned around. No mist; no spectral ship; no ghoulish, cutlass-wielding crew; and no Captain Kidd.

But no treasure, either. Mrs. Rose recounted: "Cautiously the party revisited the scene of their digging. They found their tools scattered about the summit as they had dropped them; there was a deep excavation in the earth, but no signs of an iron pot or of a smooth cavity at the bottom of the hole in which a pot might have rested."

Mrs. Rose ended her story in classic fashion, noting that none has dared search for Captain Kidd's treasure since. In what appears to be an attempt to counter the reader's incredulity at such a tale, the *New York Times* ended its report saying, "It is a matter of history that Block Island was a favorite resort of Kidd's in the closing years of his career."

Well, that settles it then.

THE DARK TALE OF WICKED WILLIAM ROSE

In the fairy tale of "Beauty and the Beast" a father makes a terrible bargain: threatened with death at the hands of a fearsome monster, he barters his beloved daughter to spare his life. The man's transgression was the theft of a single rose from the beast's garden.

A seasoned reader of fairy tales has some sympathy for the guy. Clearly, he's been set up in that familiar "guy gets lost in an enchanted wood and all hell breaks loose" kind of a way. The events leading up to the confrontation had led the man to believe that he could do as he wished at the beast's estate. It was like he was at a one-man frat party. His every wish and every whim had been fulfilled, after all. Thirsty? Here's a big goblet of mulled wine. Hungry? Try the turkey leg. Cold? Here's a fur-trimmed, satin-lined robe. Tired? Try the big bed in the master suite. And don't forget to check out the hot tub.

The man hadn't meant any harm when he happened upon the beast's sumptuous manor at the end of a long day's travel. And the house had treated him well, giving him everything he had desired. And who was there to ask permission of, anyway, in the matter of the rose? The old man hadn't seen a soul since he'd arrived. So the guy thinks it's likely no big deal to take one perfect rose from the garden to give to his daughter.

Wrong move. With the snap of the stem comes an inhuman roar and then, the creature. The boar-headed beast accuses the man of taking advantage of his hospitality. The old man quakes in fear, pleading for his life, explaining that all his lovely, virginal and altogether virtuous daughter wanted, souvenir-wise, was a single rose from her father when he returned home from his business trip. The beast has an idea. Beauty's life for her father's? The bargain is struck. And the reader is indignant. What kind of man would give his daughter over to a monster?

Well, William R. Rose, for one. Yes, Rose. Too unbelievable for fiction? Certainly. But this is the truth. According to the genealogical records of the Rose family, compiled by Ruth B. Torbert, William R. Rose of Saunderstown was the poor relation of the highly regarded Roses of Kingston. Members of this distinguished group brought honor to the family name on the battlefield and in business. William was that family member tolerated at weddings and funerals but otherwise avoided. Everybody has one, though not many families have one like William.

Torbert included in the family history a letter about Rose and his daughter, Phebe, written by Deda Macdonald, another of his daughters. The following story is Macdonald's recollection of what happened to her sister.

A Devil's Dowry

Rose was a man with few material assets. What he did have was a lovely daughter, Phebe, "a well developed and pretty miss at the tender age of 12," in 1865. His neighbor, seventy-three-year-old farmer James Gardiner, needed a wife, as he had a large house to care for and no one to help him.

Torbert described Gardiner's home in some detail: "It was an old time country house, with a huge chimney and cupboards etc. all around it." This becomes a significant detail later on.

The seventy-three-year-old geezer offered to buy the twelve-year-old Phebe from her father for $100, provided that Rose could get his girl to agree to the marriage. Wouldn't want her to feel forced, after all. "Rose took the money and the daughter went to marry the old man, of whom she was afraid, and sent under protest," Torbert wrote.

Unlike her fairy-tale counterpart, who went to the Beast willingly, Phebe wanted nothing to do with Farmer Gardiner and his monstrous proposal. Torbert continued: "When it was time for the marriage to take place, Phebe could not be found. Of course the old man was 'put out' and wanted the money back. Rose reluctantly returned the money. Phebe had hidden in the back of the old chimney. Was this white slavery? Later, under the cover of darkness, she returned to her folks and lived a normal life." Or did she?

The very next thing Torbert wrote would seem to contradict what came before: "The marriage of Phebe to James Gardiner was recorded on 5-10-1865, but some said it was a marriage by word and not by deed, as she hid from the old man."

It's a mystery as to whether Phebe became Mrs. James Gardiner in the biblical sense. What is known is that three years later, dad had married her off again. This time Phebe, now practically past her prime at fifteen, married James Caswell, "a sea-faring man, and lived happily ever after." Really, it says that.

As for William R. Rose, there are only a few other details in the genealogy. He was uncertain of his birthplace and birth year. Rose guessed that he was born in Jamestown or Newport in 1827. In 1885, it appears that he lived apart from his wife, Phebe Ann Carr Rose. William lived at Rose Hill, Storm, while wife Phebe lived with daughter Phebe and James Caswell in Saunderstown, "near the ferry slip," another detail of significance later in this story.

William Rose died in 1902.

There is one more thing. Lest you think that Rose could do no worse than sell his twelve-year-old to a seventy-three-year-old, consider Torbert's last words on the man: "There were some unpleasant notes about William Rose, but there seems no point to noting them here."

And we are left to wonder. What could a man so reprehensible as William Rose do to top himself? How about unearthing his children's corpses for the purpose of desecrating their bodies?

Rhode Island: The Ocean (of Blood) State

Here's a little-known fact: Rhode Island is the unofficial Transylvania of North America. Truly. The Ocean State boasts more recorded cases of alleged vampirism than any other state in the country (though New Hampshire is rumored to be in contention for the distinction).

Vampire folklore in America developed in conjunction with the tuberculosis epidemic that accounted for one in every four deaths in 1800, according to folklorist Michael Bell's *Food for the Dead: On the Trail of New England's Vampires*. Called consumption in the sixteenth and seventeenth centuries, tuberculosis felled entire families. Fear of the disease was great, and people grew to dread its herald: a persistent cough. Bell wrote:

> *The cough, frequent and bothersome in its early stages, became chronic with hollow rattles. An initial ruddiness of the face gave way to a deathlike pallor, which, at the very last stages of the disease, was masked by a glowing feverish flush. The mucus discharge changed color and texture from green to blood-streaked. As hemorrhaging became more frequent, the bloody discharge was measured first by teaspoons, then by cups.*

In the dark days that preceded science and rational explanations of the nature of infectious disease, people linked sickness with punishment—God's wrath, to be specific. A dissolute life invited the disease. Unhallowed habits included "too much sex, overindulgence of food, drink or tobacco, unconventional behavior, lack of exercise" and even dancing, Bell wrote.

What does all of this have to do with our William Rose? Maybe nothing. But a September 5, 1872 *Providence Herald* article titled "A Strange Story of Superstition" offered a tale of a William Rose of Saunderstown who dug up a son and a daughter at Watson's Corner, near the Saugatucket River in South Kingstown:

> *The family of Mr. William Rose, who reside at Saunderstown near the South Ferry, are subject to the consumption, several members of the family having died of the disease, and one member of the family is now quite low with it. At the urgent request of the sick man, the father, assisted by Charles Harrington of North Kingston [sic], repaired to the family burying-ground, which is located near Watson's Corner, one mile north of Peacedale [sic], and after building a fire, first dug up the grave of his son, who had been buried twelve years, for the purpose of taking out his heart and liver, which were to be placed in the fire and consumed, in order to carry out the old superstition that the consumptive dead draw nourishment from the living.*

Folk remedies for consumption often called for the extraction of vital organs from the corpse. These organs were then burned and the ashes disposed of, although sometimes a tincture was made of them and then fed to those family members battling the disease. In effect, the prevailing thought was that health could be restored to the living if the living should feed on the dead that had been feeding on the living. It's complicated. Take a minute.

Back to the *Herald* account:

> *But as the body [of the son] was entirely reduced to ashes, except a few bones, it was shortly covered up, and the body of a daughter who had been dead seven years, was taken up out of the grave beside her brother. This body was found to be nearly wasted away, except the vital parts, the liver and heart, which were in a perfect state of preservation.*

Most cases of alleged vampirism in Rhode Island involved young girls in the role of the roving revenant. The *Herald* continued:

> *The coffin also was nearly perfect, while the son's coffin was nearly demolished. After the liver and heart had been taken out of the body, it was placed in the fire and consumed, the ashes only being put back in the grave. The fire was then put out, and the two men departed to their respective homes. Only a few spectators were there to witness the horrible scene.*

Yes, witnesses. Because while ghoulish, what Rose did was not necessarily something of which his neighbors would disapprove. In fact, it may be that Rose had to show others that he was doing all that he could to deal with the problem. Twenty years later, in 1892, another well-publicized case of a father exhuming his child's remains made headlines around the world. In 1892, the body of nineteen-year-old Mercy Brown was disinterred. Her heart was removed and burned in her father's presence. Then, too, there were witnesses, including a medical doctor. These weren't isolated incidents.

The 1872 *Herald* article referred to still more incidents: "A few years ago the same was done in the village of Mooresfield, and also in the town of North Kingstown, both of course without success." Of course.

So it would appear that William R. Rose's exhumation of his long-dead children could be what Torbert was referencing in her use of the euphemism "unpleasant notes"—except for one thing: the genealogy attributed the exhumation to William *C.* Rose. Torbert quoted a July 24, 1977 *Westerly Sun* article entitled "19th Century Rhode Islanders Lived in Fear of Vampire Attacks" that claimed that

> *William C. Rose of Peace Dale feared an attack by vampires in 1874 because of his daughter's recent death. The 53-year-old man exhumed his daughter's body in Rose Hill Cemetery just outside of Kingston on Rte. 138 and "burned her heart" to avoid even the possibility of vampirism," according to a descendant of Rose. The graves of Rose and his wife Mary A. stand out prominently in the graveyard just inside*

the iron gates, but the grave of the daughter cannot be found. A search of marriage and death records in the S.K. [South Kingstown] Town Hall showed no record of the family.

Is the *Providence Herald* to be believed? Or is the *Sun* more credible? Complicating things even further, the genealogy attributed the sale of Phebe to William R. Rose and the exhumation to William C. Rose. The *Herald's* version noted that the boy and girl exhumed were the "family of Mr. William Rose, who resides at Saunderstown near the South Ferry." William R. Rose's daughter, Phebe Rose Gardiner Caswell, lived with her mother "in Saunderstown, near the ferry slip," according to the genealogy. The *Sun's* version noted that Rose was a Peace Dale resident.

Are these, then, the stories of two different men bearing almost the same name? It's unlikely but not impossible.

One final note: historical records reveal an unmarked cemetery on private property in the vicinity of Watson's Corner and the Saugatucket River that could be the one referred to in the *Herald* article. It is the final resting place of members of the family of Ebenezer Adams, grandfather of one William R. Rose of Saunderstown, who, according to 1860 U.S. Census records, was father of six children, two of whom, John and Maria, cannot be found in any Rose family cemetery in either South or North Kingstown. The children's mother, Phebe, rests at Elm Grove Cemetery in North Kingstown, with her other children, including Phebe Rose Gardiner Caswell. But not John and Maria. The 1860 census appears to be the last record of the pair. At that time, they were fifteen and four years old, respectively. The burial records of William R. Rose have not been found, either.

Could this be the cemetery by the Saugatucket River where the children's bodies were unearthed and their vital organs burned? Is the grandson of Ebenezer Adams the same William R. Rose who married his twelve-year-old daughter to his seventy-three-year-old crony? It's likely, but this cemetery isn't about to reveal any of its secrets.

Most of its headstones are unmarked or worn away.

THE SOUTH COUNTY SLAVERS

Ten million slaves crossed that ocean
They had shackles on their legs
Food goes bad, food looks rancid
But they ate it any way
Don't know where, where they're going
Don't know where, where they've been
Don't know where, where they're going
Don't know where, where they've been

— "Ten Million Slaves," Otis Taylor

Usually when discussing slavery in the Ocean State, the talk turns to Providence and Newport and to the Browns, the DeWolfs and the Vernons. But it didn't just happen there.

In the state's southernmost county, Washington County, nicknamed South County, traces of its bygone colonial charms still delight. Its best features: the clapboard colonials of Wickford, the lichen-laced stone walls of Matunuck and the brine-sharpened air of Narragansett. All enchant tourists and remind natives how lucky they are to live there.

Washington County wasn't the original name given to this place. Until 1782, it was King's County. No doubt those who proposed the name change wanted to free themselves of the yoke of monarchy. It would take a little longer, though, for these same people to shed the tyranny in themselves.

It may surprise some people to learn that this area of the state depended on slave labor to support itself. It surprised historian Joanne Pope Melish, who wrote in her 1988 book *Disowning Slavery: Gradual Emancipation and "Race" in New England 1780–1860*:

> *It was in Rhode Island, where I lived after 1964, that I first stumbled across an obscure reference to local slavery, but almost no one I asked knew anything about it. Members of the historical society did, but they assured me that slavery in Rhode Island had been brief and benign, involving only the best families, who behaved with genteel kindness.*

They pointed me in the direction of several antiquarian histories, which said about the same thing.

Wow. Makes you wonder who wrote those charming antiquarian histories replete with tales of "the best families, who behaved with genteel kindness."

In *Runaways, Deserters, and Notorious Villains*, authors Maureen Alice Taylor and John Wood Sweet examine ads that ran in Rhode Island newspapers in the eighteenth century. A 1799 notice in the *Newport Mercury*, reprinted in the book, contradicts what the historical society members told Melish:

ON the 15ᵗʰ of this inst. June, a Negro Wench went from me, named FLORA, about 34 or 35 Years of Age, a short, squaddy-built Wench; had on, when she went away, a green Quilt, and a dark Calico short Gown, and Bonnet; and carried with her a light Calico Gown, and a striped green, and two short Gowns; one Calico, the other striped; and three Pair of Shoes, four or five Pair of Stockings, and five or six Handkerchiefs, with sundry other Articles of Cloating; and I have heard, she went into an House and told them, she never intended to come back again:—Therefore, for her Behavior, I hereby forewarn any Person or Persons employing or harbouring her, in any Way whatever, on Penalty of the Law. Daniel Sunderland.

Yeah, Daniel Sunderland sounds genteel.

Historian Douglas Harper offered a myth-busting explanation of why slavery did not flourish here:

The North failed to develop large-scale agrarian slavery, such as later arose in the Deep South, but that had little to do with morality and much to do with climate and economy. The elements which characterized Southern slavery in the 19ᵗʰ century, and which New England abolitionists claimed to view with abhorrence, all were present from an early date in the North. Practices such as the breeding of slaves like animals for market, or the crime of slave mothers killing their infants, testify that slavery's brutalizing force was at work in New England.

Otis Taylor puts it succinctly: "Rain and fire crossed that ocean/ Another mad man done struck again."

The Economics of Slavery

Harper argues that colonization and slavery go hand in hand. "Every New World colony was, in some sense, a slave colony," he wrote. "French Canada, Massachusetts, Rhode Island, Pennsylvania, Virginia, Cuba, Brazil—all of them made their start in an economic system built upon slavery based on race."

In southern Rhode Island, the running of the area's large commercial dairy farms required slave labor, wrote Christopher McBurney in his preface to *Jailed for Preaching: The Story of Cato Pearce, a Freed Slave from Washington County, Rhode Island*:

> *The so-called Narragansett planters on the average held about 400 sheep, 100 dairy cows and other cattle, and 20 horses. They traded cheese, butter, horses, sheep and other farm products to nearby Newport merchants. They had slaves clear their lands for farming, tend to the herds, plant and harvest crops, help to transport goods and run errands to Newport, and perform domestic service in their houses. Narragansett planters each held from five to twenty slaves.*

It was the Quakers in the area who first pointed out that the keeping of slaves was incompatible with a budding, and treasonous, colonial philosophy that prized individual freedom. Quakers called the Narragansett Friends denied membership to slave owners. And in 1771, female members of this congregation formed a committee that visited congregants to see who among them held slaves. Those in possession of slaves faced expulsion from the Friends. In an 1899 book titled *The Narragansett Friends' Meeting in the 18ᵗʰ Century With a Chapter on Quaker Beginnings in Rhode Island*, author Caroline Hazard reproduces the minutes of the meeting, including this entry concerning a female slave owner soon to be served her eviction notice:

She is denied her membership, as of late it doth appear that She hath Refused to comply with that part of our Discipline which is against the enslaving [of] Mankind a Practice very repugnant to the Truth and Equity an invation [sic] of the Natural Rights of Mankind subjecting them to a state of Bondage and oppression wholly inconsistent with the Spirit of the Gospel.

These women were serious about their work. Within two years, they reported that no congregants owned slaves.

Hazard wrote of one local man's reversal on the subject of slavery in "Rowland Robinson's Repentance." In the ballad, Rowland Robinson awaits a slave ship bearing twenty-eight people he's purchased. Those awaiting the ship's arrival are merry, greeting one another warmly and laughing as they await their cargo. Hazard wrote that it was

[a] prosperous voyage of just thirty days
Across from the Guinea coast;
The rum was all gone, and very good trade,
Such was the proud Captain's boast.
He spoke not of the shark
That was fed after dark
And followed all day at his post.

Robinson's merriment turns to horror as he beholds the ship's passengers:

And the light of the sun beheld the foul sight,
Close packed, between decks, there they lay,
And the only room they ever had had
Was when corpses were taken away.
Most ghastly the sight
When seen in the light
Of the sun that shone at midday.

Weak, starving, and feeble, and quaking with fear,
Naked, unable to stand,

Half dead, and wounded, and covered with filth,
The cargo was brought to the land.
And the laugh died away,
In the company gay,
As they saw that piteous band.

Rowland Robinson swore 'tis was a sin and shame;
His laughter rang gaily no more,
As he listened and looked with horrified gaze,
And worse terrors came than before;
And his curses were wild,
Then he sobbed like a child,
And his tears drowned the oaths that he swore.

Vermont was the first New England state to officially outlaw slavery in 1777. Massachusetts and New Hampshire followed suit in 1783. Connecticut came round a year later, as did Rhode Island, though by degrees.

In 1784, Rhode Island enacted a law emancipating those born on or after March 1, 1784. The parents of those children, however, stayed slaves under the law. Moreover, an amendment to the law stipulated that the owners of slaves with children would be allowed to keep them until they reached adulthood—twenty-one years of free labor. Then the slave children were given their freedom.

Life for a freed slave was not easy. In South Kingstown, freedmen were barred from owning horses and other livestock. It would be some time before the community came round to treating former slaves with respect.

Swamp Yankee and Proud of It

Swamp Yankee. Some think it a pejorative term, one used for cowards who took to the swamps in 1776 to avoid tangling with British soldiers. Others say that they think it was a name given to South County residents in the 1920s by northern Rhode Islanders, city types, who thought that anyone living beyond the East Greenwich border was ignorant and uncouth.

A roadside farm stand's warning. *Photo by author.*

At some point, though, what was intended as insult became a badge of honor, something earned by those few families who could trace their lineage back to the area's most prominent families, like the Hazards, the Gardiners and the Sweets. All others are forever outsiders. Less stuffy than the Boston Brahmins, Swamp Yankees are more like Maine's Down Easters: good folk of few words, reliable, thrifty and uncaring about what others may say of them. They'd bristle at the idea that they were elitist; that would imply that Swamp Yankees formed some kind of group or association, and this goes against their essential rugged individualism. Swamp Yankees don't exclude; they just don't engage. Award-winning author John Casey in his novel *Compass Rose* has newcomer Phoebe Fitzgerald lay it all out:

> *How long does a person have to live here to really live here? It's been three years and people still say, "So you staying on past Labor Day again?" It's as if there are things you have to know but that nobody tells you…I'll be a newcomer until I'm old and gray…I'm usually good at*

fitting in. I like getting to know people and having people get to know me. But around here it's as if everyone already knows what they need to know, and what's the point of talking about it.

The woman to whom Phoebe is speaking, a kind local woman named May, tries to explain that the offense, while real, is not personal, which may just be worse. "There's some truth in that...but it doesn't mean they're thinking about you one way or the other," May tells Phoebe.

Ouch.

History of the Term

The term's origins are a mystery. A 2008 *Providence Journal* article titled "Is 'Swamp Yankee' an Insult or a Badge of Honor?" quoted one reader who was incensed at the use of the term in print. The man said that "Swamp Yankee" was "a derogatory term used by the so-called 'enlightened' city dwellers in reference to people who live in more rural settings in this part of the country."

One scholar concurs. Ruth Schell says the term was first used to describe New Englanders who slunk into the swamps during the American Revolution rather than face British soldiers. When the threat had passed, the cowards returned and found themselves shunned by those who'd stayed to defend their homes. And so Swamp Yankee became synonymous with cowardice. With time, the definition of the term became more expansive to include other vices. Swamp Yankees were shiftless, unfriendly, stubborn, penurious, suspicious of outsiders and backward thinking. As if.

The *Journal* writer sought out well-known and respected South County residents for their opinions. On balance, they said, the contemporary view of the term is that it is a status many admire but few achieve. "If you're a Swamp Yankee, it means your family's been here for hundreds of years," Rhode Island cartoonist Don Bousquet told the *Journal* reporter. "And Swamp Yankees are like cowboys, like Gary Cooper. They talk with a twang, if they talk at all."

Say "Swamp Yankee," and those of the same mind as Bousquet will rattle off adjectives like reliable, resourceful, thrifty, self-reliant and smart.

Maybe not smart in the way of a professor, mind you, but how many PhDs would be able to feed themselves if first they had to hunt and gather?

Swamp Yankees could put together a clambake without having to go to a grocery store—though, for corn on the cob and potatoes, they might patronize a roadside family farm stand. As long as it's the kind that employs a low-tech, honor-system payment method: cashing out via a tin can with a coin slot cut in its plastic top.

There are some who even believe that the term has a certain cachet. Two novels with the title *Swamp Yankee* have been written and there are songs, including "Swamp Yankees" by Foxtrot Zulu and "Swamp Yankees in Paradise" by the swing band the Swamp Yankees. And the Chariho Rotary Club has been hosting "Swamp Yankee Days" at Crandall Field in Ashaway since 1992. Events include a tractor parade, square dancing, a Mr. and Mrs. Swamp Yankee contest, fiddling, a baked bean–eating contest and cow chip bingo.

For those outsiders unfamiliar with the latter, cow chip bingo involves setting a few well-fed cows on a grassy grid and laying bets on which one relieves itself first. Only a Swamp Yankee would see the gaming potential in a pungent pile of steaming manure.

Thrift takes many forms.

Joshua Tefft:
Drawn and Quartered in South County

If bad deaths could be set on a spectrum, being drawn and quartered would fall somewhere between being drowned in sewage and being eaten by rats.

The English are credited with inventing drawing and quartering in about 1351 or so for those convicted of high treason. To the English, high treason, like high tea, was a big deal and warranted big punishment. The whole execution thing started simply enough: the traitor to the Crown was lashed to a woven wooden pallet, called a hurdle, and drawn through the streets to the place of his death. A bumpy ride was the least of it.

The traitor was hanged *almost* to the point of death. Then his executioners revived him via emasculation and disembowelment before

Smith's Castle, North Kingstown, site of the execution of Joshua Tefft. *Photo by author.*

the eventual beheading. Then his corpse was quartered, yes, as in cut into four pieces. Still not done yet, though. In this pre-billboard era, traitorous limbs and torsos were used as advertisements on British landmarks, like the London Bridge. Just a friendly little PSA from your local monarch of what awaited insurgents daft enough to challenge the king.

It bears mention here that the English felt that common decency forbade the drawing and quartering of women. They were burned instead. Much more genteel.

In America, there is only one instance of the drawing and quartering of a man for treason. And, it should be noted, different accounts tell the story differently. Joshua Teft or Tefft, depending upon the version, was executed for fighting on the side of the Narragansetts in the Great Swamp Fight of December 19, 1675. Tefft, called Hatchet Tefft in one version of the story, was a white man who married a Wampanoag woman in 1662. Accounts agree that he forfeited his ties to the community of his birth and elected instead to live near his wife's people. How he became involved in the Great

Swamp Fight, which resulted in the deaths of between six hundred and seven hundred Narragansetts and the imprisonment of another three hundred, is debatable. One version of the story casts him as a renegade, a Narragansett sympathizer. Another story has Tefft telling his captor, Captain Fenner of Providence, that he was coerced into fighting for the Narragansetts.

Leo Bonfanti's book *Biographies and Legends of the New England Indians* offers the most extensive account I have found of Tefft's trial and execution. In it, Tefft was captured on January 14, 1675, by a Captain Fenner of Providence, tried by an army court and found guilty of treason. In his defense, Tefft told the court that he'd been abducted by the Narragansetts and forced, upon pain of death, to work on their fortress. Further, he told the court that the colonists were being deceived by the various indigenous tribes. The Pequots and the Mohicans only appeared to have taken the side of the British in this conflict, Tefft said. Tefft argued that the three tribes were actually in league with one another. He noted the Pequots and

North Kingstown's Smith's Castle also has a memorial marker honoring the forty colonists killed in the Great Swamp Fight. *Photo by author.*

The Smith's Castle sign, North Kingstown. *Photo by author.*

Mohicans had only feigned fighting, deliberately missing when shooting at the Narragansetts.

Despite this and other allegations of duplicitous behavior on the part of the Native Americans, the court was unmoved. In fact, the most damning evidence against Tefft was his apostasy, his abandoning of his own people in favor of those of his wife. According to Bonfanti, he was found guilty and shot, and "Because of his background, his body was quartered and left unburied."

Edgar Mahew Bacon concurs with Bonfanti, casting Joshua Tefft as a homicidal renegade "who had fled from Massachusetts after the commission of crime and took refuge with the Narragansetts." Bacon, the author of *Narragansett Bay: Its Historic and Romantic Associations*, wrote:

> *War between the races was then in progress and in order to show the genuineness of his apostasy he stained his hands with a white man's blood, bringing to the Narragansett camp the scalp of a miller whom*

he had surprised and slain. It was commonly believed that Tefft had killed both his father and his mother. To this man was attributed the planning of the swamp fortress, or fortified camp, that for so long made the Narragansetts almost invulnerable against the attacks of the settlers.

Another version of the Tefft story has the historic landmark Smith's Castle in North Kingstown as the site of the execution. In *Plantation in Yankeeland*, author Carl R. Woodward's account of events, Tefft is wounded, apprehended and interrogated by Rhode Island's own religious freedom rock star Roger Williams. Williams, friend to Indian and white alike, must have had a difficult time with the case. The original civil liberties champion, Williams respected New England's native peoples and believed that European immigrants should have the right to practice whatever religion they saw fit. What must Williams have thought of the Tefft case? Unfortunately, Woodward doesn't tell us, casting Tefft as

a renegade white known as Hatchet Tefft, who married a squaw and lived with the Indians. Fighting on their side in the swamp battle he was wounded in the knee, but escaped. About four weeks later in an encounter near Providence, he was captured and made prisoner. He was thoroughly quizzed by Roger Williams who sent a full report of the examination to Governor Leverett at Boston. It appears that Tefft was then taken to Smith's Castle where he was condemned to die the death of a traitor. One tradition has it that he was hanged on a gatepost on the green between the house and the road, another that he suffered the horrible penalty and supreme disgrace of being "drawn and quartered."

What became of Tefft's body is unknown, and there is no marker to note his death. There is, however, a plaque marking the mass grave of forty colonists who lost their lives in the Great Swamp Fight.

You have to wonder what Roger Williams thought of the proceedings. Puritan society allowed Williams his friendship with the Narragansetts, but it seems that Tefft's apostasy was unforgiveable.

Bibliography

Allen, Frederick Lewis. *Only Yesterday: An Informal History of the 1920s.* New York: Harper & Row, 1964.

Bell, Michael E. *Food for the Dead: On the Trail of New England's Vampires.* New York: Carroll & Graf, 2001.

Bonfanti, Leo. *Biographies and Legends of the New England Indians.* Wakefield, MA: Pride Publications, 1971.

Caldwell, Charles. *Memoirs of the Life and Campaigns of the Hon. Nathaniel Greene Major General in the Army of the United States and Commander of the Southern Department in the War of the Revolution.* Philadelphia, PA: Robert Desilver and Thomas Desilver, 1819.

Carbone, Gerald M. *Nathanael Greene: A Biography of the American Revolution.* New York: Palgrave Macmillan, 2008.

Chapin, Howard M. *Report Upon the Burial Place of Roger Williams.* Providence: Rhode Island Historical Society, 1918.

Crouch, Andy. *The Good Beer Guide to New England.* Hanover, NH: University Press of New England, 2006.

Davis, Deborah. *Gilded: How Newport Became America's Richest Resort.* Hoboken, NJ: Wiley, 2009.

Dorough, Bob. "Mother Necessity." *Schoolhouse Rock* television program, 1977.

Dow, George Francis, and John Henry Edmonds. *The Pirates of the New England Coast, 1630–1730.* New York: Dover Publications, 1996.

Drake, James David. *King Philip's War: Civil War in New England, 1675–1676.* Amherst: University of Massachusetts Press, 1999.

Eddy, Muriel E., C.M. Eddy and Jim Dyer. *The Gentleman from Angell Street: Memories of H.P. Lovecraft.* Narragansett, RI: Fenham Publishing, 2001.

Gilbert Stuart: Portraitist of the Young Republic. Providence: Rhode Island School of Design, 1967.

Greene, George Washington. *A Short History of Rhode Island.* Providence, RI: J.A. & R.A. Reid, 1877.

Griswold, S.S. *1757 Historical Sketch of the Town of Hopkinton From 1757 to 1876, Comprising a Period of 119 Years.* Hope Valley, RI: L.W.A. Cole, 1877.

Hale, Edward Everett. *The Man without a Country.* Gloucester, UK: Dodo, 2008.

Hazard, Caroline. *Narragansett Ballads.* New York: Houghton Mifflin & Co., 1894.

————. *Narragansett Friends' Meeting in the 18ᵗʰ Century With a Chapter on Quaker Beginnings in Rhode Island*. New York: Houghton, Mifflin & Co., 1900.

James, Henry. "An International Episode." Pennsylvania State University. http//www2.hn.psu.edu/faculty/jmanis/jimspdf.htm.

James, Henry, and T.J. Lustig. *The Turn of the Screw and Other Stories*. Oxford: Oxford University Press, 2008.

Lehnert, Tim. *Rhode Island 101: Everything You Wanted to Know about Rhode Island and Were Going to Ask Anyway*. Lunenburg, NS, Canada: MacIntyre Purcell Publishing, 2009.

Lippincott, Bertram. *Indians, Privateers, and High Society: A Rhode Island Sampler*. Philadelphia, PA: Lippincott, 1961.

McBurney, Christian M. *A History of Kingston, R.I., 1700–1900: Heart of Rural South County*. Kingston, RI: Pettaquamscutt Historical Society, 2004.

McBurney, Christopher. *Jailed for Preaching: The Story of Cato Pearce, a Freed Slave from Washington County, Rhode Island*. Kingston, RI: Pettaquamscutt Historical Society, 2006.

McLanathan, Richard B.K. *Gilbert Stuart*. New York: Abrams, in Association with National Museum of American Art, Smithsonian Institution, 1986.

Melish, Joanne Pope. *Disowning Slavery: Gradual Emancipation and "Race" in New England, 1780–1860*. Ithaca, NY: Cornell University Press, 1998.

Oates, Joyce Carol. "The King of Weird." *New York Review of Books*, October 31, 1996.

Patten, David. "Those Four Corner Ladies." Reprinted in *A Patchwork History of Tiverton, Rhode Island*. Tiverton, RI: Tiverton Historical Society, 1976.

Pettaquamscutt Chapter of the Daughters of the American Revolution. *Facts and Fancies Concerning North Kingstown Rhode Island*. Pawtucket, RI: Globe Printing, 1989.

Providence Herald. "A Strange Story of Superstition." September 5, 1872.

Ritchie, Ethel Colt. *Block Island Lore and Legends*. Block Island, RI: F. Norman Associates, 1955.

Rybicki, Verena. "The Mill Girls of Lowell." *The Traditional Quilter*, September and November 1990. Reprinted in *The Lowell Mill Girls: Life in the Factory*. Edited by JoAnne W. Deitch. Carlisle, MA: Discovery Enterprises, 1998.

Taylor, Maureen A. *Runaways, Deserters, and Notorious Villains*. Rockland, ME: Picton Press, 2001.

Taylor, Otis. "Ten Million Slaves." *Recapturing the Banjo*, 2008. CD.

Visit Historic Savannah. www.visit-historic-savannah.com.

Vowell, Sarah. *The Wordy Shipmates*. New York: Riverhead, 2008.

Westerly Sun. "19th Century Rhode Islanders Lived in Fear of Vampire Attacks." July 24, 1977.

Williams, Roger. *A Key Into the Language of America*. Detroit, MI: Wayne State University Press, 1973.

Wohleber, Curt. "The Man Who Can Scare Stephen King." *American Heritage Magazine* 46, issue 8 (December 1995).

Woodward, Carl R. *Plantation in Yankeeland.* Chester, CT: Pequot Press, Inc., 1971.

Workers of the Federal Writers' Project of the Works Progress Administration for the State of Rhode Island. *Rhode Island a Guide to the Smallest State.* Boston, MA: Houghton Mifflin, 1937.

About the Author

M.E. Reilly-McGreen is a wife and mother of three. A former journalist and high school English teacher, she is currently a content strategist at Embolden, a website design, development and consulting firm in Pawtucket, Rhode Island. *Revolutionaries, Rebels and Rogues of Rhode Island* is the follow-up to her first book: *Witches, Wenches and Wild Women of Rhode Island* (The History Press, 2010).

Photo by Mark Kiely.

Visit us at
www.historypress.net